Python *from the very beginning*

In *Python from the Very Beginning* John Whitington takes a no-prerequisites approach to teaching a modern general-purpose programming language. Each small, self-contained chapter introduces a new topic, building until the reader can write quite substantial programs. There are plenty of questions and, crucially, worked answers and hints.

Python from the Very Beginning will appeal both to new programmers, and to experienced programmers eager to explore a new language. It is suitable both for formal use within an undergraduate or graduate curriculum, and for the interested amateur.

JOHN WHITINGTON founded a company which sells software for document processing. He taught programming to students of Computer Science at the University of Cambridge. His other books include the textbooks *"PDF Explained"* (O'Reilly, 2012), *"OCaml from the Very Beginning"* (Coherent, 2013), and *"Haskell from the Very Beginning"* (Coherent, 2019) and the Popular Science book *"A Machine Made this Book: Ten Sketches of Computer Science"* (Coherent, 2016).

PYTHON

from the very beginning

John Whitington

COHERENT PRESS

C O H E R E N T P R E S S

Cambridge

Published in the United Kingdom by Coherent Press, Cambridge

© Coherent Press 2020

First published October 2020

A catalogue record for this book is available from the British Library

ISBN 978-0-9576711-5-7 Paperback

by the same author

PDF Explained (O'Reilly, 2012)
OCaml from the Very Beginning (Coherent, 2013)
More OCaml: Methods, Algorithms & Diversions (Coherent, 2014)
A Machine Made this Book: Ten Sketches of Computer Science (Coherent, 2016)
Haskell from the Very Beginning (Coherent, 2019)

Contents

Getting Ready   ix

1   Starting Off   1

2   Names and Functions   11

Using Scripts   21

3   Again and Again   23

4   Making Lists   33

5   More with Lists and Strings   45

6   Prettier Printing   55

7   Arranging Things   63

8   When Things Go Wrong   75

9   More with Files   85

10   The Other Numbers   95

11   The Standard Library   105

12   Building Bigger Programs   111

Project 1: Pretty Pictures   117

Project 2: Counting Calories   131

Project 3: Noughts and Crosses   139

Project 4: Photo Finish   147

Answers to Questions   153

Hints for Questions   221

Index   227

Preface

I have tried to write a book which has no prerequisites – and with which any intelligent person ought to be able to cope, whilst trying to be concise enough that a programmer experienced in another language might not be too annoyed by the pace or tone.

This may well not be the last book you read on Python, but one of the joys of Python is that substantial, useful programs can be constructed quickly from a relatively small set of constructs. There is enough in this book to build such useful programs, as we see in the four extended projects.

Answers and Hints are at the back of the book.

Chapters

In chapter 1 we begin our exploration of Python with a series of preliminaries, introducing ways to calculate with the whole numbers, compare them with one another, and print them out. We learn about *truth values* and the other types of simple data which Python supports.

In chapter 2 we build little Python programs of our own, using *functions* to perform calculations based on changing inputs. We make decisions using conditional constructs to choose differing courses of action.

In chapter 3 we learn about Python constructs which perform actions repeatedly, for a fixed number of times or until a certain condition is met. We start to build larger, more useful programs, including interactive ones which depend upon input from the keyboard.

In chapter 4 we begin to build and manipulate larger pieces of data by combining things into lists, and querying and processing them. This increases considerably the scope of programs we can write.

In chapter 5 we expand our work with lists to manipulate strings, splitting them into words, processing them, and putting them back together. We learn how to sort lists into order, and how to build lists from scratch using *list comprehensions*.

In chapter 6 we learn more about printing messages and data to the screen, and use this knowledge to print nicely-formatted tables of data. We learn how to write such data to a file on the computer, instead of to the screen.

In chapter 7 we learn another way of storing data – in *dictionaries* which allow us to build little databases, looking up data by searching for it by name. We also work with *sets*, which allow us to store collections of data without repetition, in the same way as mathematical sets do.

In chapter 8 we deal with the thorny topic of errors: what do we do when an input is unexpected? When we find a number when we were expecting a list? When an item is not found in a dictionary? We learn how to report, handle, and recover from these errors.

In chapter 9 we return to the subject of files, learning how to read from them as well as write to them, and illustrate with a word counting program. We deal with errors, such as the unexpected absence of a file.

In chapter 10 we talk about real numbers, which we have avoided thus far. We show how to calculate with the trigonometric functions and how to convert between whole and real numbers by rounding.

In chapter 11 we introduce the Python Standard Library, greatly expanding the pre-built components at our disposal. We learn how to look up functions in Python's official documentation.

In chapter 12 we build stand-alone programs which can be run from the command line, as if they were built in to the computer. We are now ready to begin on larger projects.

Projects

In project 1 we draw all sorts of pretty pictures by giving the computer instructions on how to draw them line by line. We make a graph plotter and a visual clock program.

In project 2 we write a calorie-counting program which stores its data across several files, and which allows multiple users. We build an interface for it, with several different commands. We learn how to use a standard data format, so that spreadsheet programs can load our calorie data.

In project 3 we investigate the childhood game of Noughts and Crosses, writing human and computer players, and working out some statistical properties of the game by building a structure containing all possible games.

In project 4 we learn how to manipulate photographs, turning them into greyscale, blurring them, and making animations from them.

Online resources

To save typing, all the examples and exercises for this book can be found in electronic form at `https://pythonfromtheverybeginning.com`. The book's errata lives there too.

Acknowledgements

The technical reviewer provided valuable corrections and suggestions, but all mistakes remain the author's. The image on page 147 is from "Flexible Strategy Use in Young Children's Tic-Tac-Toe" by Kevin Crowley and Robert S. Siegler, and is reproduced courtesy of Elsevier.

Getting Ready

This book is about teaching the computer to do new things by writing computer programs. Just as there are different languages for humans to speak to one another, there are different *programming languages* for humans to speak to computers.

We are going to be using a programming language called **Python**. A Python system might already be on your computer, or you may have to find it on the internet and install it yourself. You will know that you have it working when you see something like this:

```
Python 3.8.2 (default, Feb 24 2020, 18:27:02)
[Clang 10.0.1 (clang-1001.0.46.4)] on darwin
Type "help", "copyright", "credits" or "license" for more information.
>>>
```

Make sure the Python version number in the first line, here Python 3.8.2, is at least 3. You might need to type `python3` instead of `python` to achieve this. Python is waiting for us to type something. Try typing `1` `space` `+` `space` `2` followed by the `Enter` key. You should see this:

```
Python
>>> 1 + 2
3
>>>
```

(We have abbreviated Python's welcome message). Python tells us the result of the calculation. You may use the left and right arrow keys on the keyboard to correct mistakes and the up and down arrow keys to look through a history of previous inputs. You can also use your computer's usual copy and paste functions, instead of typing directly into Python, if you like.

To abandon typing, and ask Python to forget what you have already typed, enter `Ctrl-C` (hold down the `Ctrl` key and tap the `c` key). This will allow you to start again. To leave Python altogether, give the `exit()` command, again followed by `Enter`:

```
Python
>>> exit()
```

You should find yourself back where you were before. We are ready to begin.

Chapter 1

Starting Off

We will cover a fair amount of material in this chapter and its questions, since we will need a solid base on which to build. You should read this with a computer running Python in front of you.

Expressions and statements

A computer program written in Python is built from *statements* and *expressions*. Each statement performs some action. For example, the built-in `print` statement writes to the screen:

```
Python
>>> print('Just like this')                  note the parentheses and single quotation marks
Just like this
```

Each expression performs some calculation, yielding a value. For example, we can calculate the result of a simple mathematical expression using whole numbers (or *integers*):

```
Python
>>> 1 + 2 * 3
7
```

When Python has calculated the result of this expression, it prints it to the screen, even though we have not used `print`. All of our programs will be built from such statements and expressions.

The single quotation marks in our `print` statement indicate that what we are printing is a *string* – a sequence of letters or other symbols. If the string is to contain a single quotation mark, we must use the double quotation mark key instead:

```
Python
>>> print('Can't use single quotation marks here!')
  File "<stdin>", line 1
    print('Can't use single quotation marks here!')
               ^
SyntaxError: invalid syntax
```

1

```
>>> print("Can't use single quotation marks here!")
Can't use single quotation marks here!
```

Note that this is a different key on the keyboard – we are not typing two single quotation marks – it is " not ' '. We can print numbers too, of course:

```
Python
>>> print(12)
12
```

Note that 12 and '12' are different things: one is the whole number (or integer) 12, and one is the string consisting of the two symbols 1 and 2. Notice also the difference between an expression which is just a string, and the statement which is the act of printing a string:

```
Python
>>> 'Just like this'
'Just like this'
>>> print('Just like this')
Just like this
```

Numbers

We have seen how to do mathematical calculations with our numbers, of course:

```
Python
>>> 1 + 2 * 3
7
```

Even quite large calculations:

```
Python
>>> 1000000000 + 2000000000 * 3000000000
6000000001000000000
```

Using the _ underscore key to split up the numbers is optional, but helps with readability:

```
Python
>>> 1_000_000_000 + 2_000_000_000 * 3_000_000_000
6000000001000000000
```

Python reduces the mathematical expression 1 + 2 * 3 to the value 7 and then prints it to the screen. This expression contains the *operators* + and * and their *operands* 1, 2, and 3.

How does Python know how to calculate 1 + 2 * 3? Following known rules, just like we would. We know that the multiplication here should be done before the addition, and so does Python. So the calculation goes like this:

$$1 + \underline{2 \times 3}$$
$$\implies \underline{1 + 6}$$
$$\implies 7$$

The piece being processed at each stage is underlined. We say that the multiplication operator has higher *precedence* than the addition operator. Here are some of Python's operators for arithmetic:

Operator	Description
$a + b$	addition
$a - b$	subtract b from a
$a * b$	multiplication

In addition to our rule about * being performed before + and -, we also need a rule to say what is meant by 9 - 4 + 1. Is it (9 - 4) + 1 which is 6, or 9 - (4 + 1) which is 4? As with normal arithmetic, it is the former in Python:

```
Python
>>> 9 - 4 + 1
6
```

This is known as the *associativity* of the operators.

Truth and falsity

Of course, there are many more things than just numbers. Sometimes, instead of numbers, we would like to talk about truth: either something is true or it is not. For this we use *boolean values*, named after the English mathematician George Boole (1815–1864) who pioneered their use. There are just two booleans:

```
True
False
```

How can we use these? One way is to use one of the *comparison operators*, which are used for comparing values to one another:

```
Python
>>> 99 > 100
False
>>> 4 + 3 + 2 + 1 == 10
True
```

It is most important not to confuse == with = as the single = symbol means something else in Python. Here are the comparison operators:

Operator	Description
$a == b$	true if a and b are equal
$a < b$	true if a is less than b
$a <= b$	true if a is less than or equal to b
$a > b$	true if a is more than b
$a >= b$	true if a is more than or equal to b
$a != b$	true if a is not equal to b

There are two operators for combining boolean values (for instance, those resulting from using the comparison operators). The expression *a* **and** *b* evaluates to True only if expressions *a* and *b* both evaluate to True. The expression *a* **or** *b* evaluates to True if *a* evaluates to True or *b* evaluates to True, or both do. Here are some examples of these operators in use:

```
Python
>>> 1 == 1 and 10 > 9
True
>>> 1 == 1 or 9 > 10
True
```

In each case, the expression *a* will be tested first – the second may not need to be tested at all. The **and** operator is performed before **or**, so *a* **and** *b* **or** *c* is the same as (*a* **and** *b*) **or** *c*. The expression **not** *a* gives True if *a* is False and vice versa:

```
Python
>>> not 1 == 1
False
>>> 1 == 2 or not 9 > 10
True
```

The comparison operators have a higher precedence than the so-called logical operators: so, for example, writing not 1 == 1 is the same as writing not (1 == 1) rather than (not 1) == 1.

The types of things

In this chapter we have seen three types of data: strings, integers and booleans. We can ask Python to tell us the type of a value or expression:

```
Python
>>> type('Hello!')
<class 'str'>
>>> type(25)
<class 'int'>
>>> type(1 + 2 * 3)
<class 'int'>
>>> type(False)
<class 'bool'>
```

Here, 'str' indicates strings, 'bool' booleans, and 'int' integers.

Common problems

When Python does not recognise what we type in as a valid program, an error message is shown instead of an answer. You will come across this many times when experimenting with your first Python programs, and part of learning to program is learning to recognise and fix these mistakes. For example, if we miss the quotation mark from the end of a string, we see this:

```
Python
>>> print('A string without a proper end)
  File "<stdin>", line 1
    print('A string without a proper end)
                                         ^
SyntaxError: EOL while scanning string literal
```

Such error messages are not always easy to understand. What is EOL? What is a literal? What is <stdin>? Nevertheless, you will become used to such messages, and how to fix your programs. In the next example, we try to compare a number to a string:

```
Python
>>> 1 < '2'
Traceback (most recent call last):
  File "<stdin>", line 1, in <module>
TypeError: '<' not supported between instances of 'int' and 'str'
```

In this case the error message is a little easier to understand. Another common situation is missing out a closing parenthesis. In this case, Python does not know we have finished typing, even when we press Enter.

```
Python
>>> 2 * (3 + 4 + 5
...
...
...
...
```

To get out of this situation, we can type Ctrl-C, to let Python know we wish to discard the statement and try again:

```
Python
>>> 2 * (3 + 4 + 5
...
...
...
...
KeyboardInterrupt
```

Or, if possible, we can finish the expression properly:

```
Python
>>> 2 * (3 + 4 + 5
...
...
...
...)
24
```

Summary

We have learned how to interact with Python by typing statements and reading the answers. We have learned about three types of data: strings, whole numbers, and booleans. We have seen how to perform arithmetic on numbers, and how to test things for equality with one another, using operators and operands. We have learned about boolean operators too. Finally, we have learned how to ask Python to tell us the type of something.

In the next chapter, we will move on to more substantial programs. Meanwhile, there are some questions to try. Answers and hints are at the back of the book.

Questions

1. What sorts of thing do the following expressions represent and to what do they evaluate, and why? See if you can work them out without the computer to begin with.

```
17
1 + 2 * 3 + 4
400 > 200
1 != 1
True or False
True and False
'%'
```

2. A programmer writes 1+2 * 3+4. What does this evaluate to? What advice would you give them?

3. Python has a modulus or remainder operator, which finds the remainder of dividing one number by another. It is written %. Consider the evaluations of the expressions 1 + 2 % 3, (1 + 2) % 3, and 1 + (2 % 3). What can you conclude about the + and % operators?

4. What is the effect of the comparison operators like < and > on strings? For example, to what does 'bacon' < 'eggs' evaluate? What about 'Bacon' < 'bacon'? What is the effect of the comparison operators on the booleans True and False?

5. What (if anything) do the following statements print on the screen? Can you work out or guess what they will do before typing them in?

```
1 + 2
'one' + 'two'
1 + 'two'
3 * '1'
'1' * 3
print('1' * 3)
True + 1
print(f'One and two is {1 + 2} and that is all.')
```

(The last of these uses Python in a way we have not yet mentioned.)

So Far

1 Strings like `'this'`. Printing to the screen with `print`. The numbers ... -3,-2,-1,0,1,2,3.... The arithmetic operators + - * and their precedence and associativity. The boolean values `True` and `False` and their operators **and**, **or**, and **not**. Comparison operators == < <= >= > !=. Finding types with `type`.

Chapter 2

Names and Functions

So far we have built only tiny toy programs. To build bigger ones, we need to be able to name things so as to refer to them later. We also need to write expressions whose result depends upon one or more other things.

Names

So far, if we wished to use a sub-expression twice or more in a single expression, we had to type it multiple times:

```Python
>>> 200 * 200 * 200
8000000
```

Instead, we can define our own name to stand for the result of evaluating an expression, and then use the name as we please:

```Python
>>> x = 200
>>> x * x * x
8000000
```

We can update the value associated with the name and try the calculation again:

```Python
>>> x = 200
>>> x * x * x
8000000
>>> x = 5 + 5
>>> x * x * x
1000
```

Because of this ability to vary the value associated with the name, things like x are called *variables*. We can use any name we like for a variable, so long as it does not clash with any of Python's built in *keywords*:

and as assert async await break class continue def del elif else except finally for from global if import in is lambda nonlocal not or pass raise return try while with yield

In Python, we use lower case letters or words for variable names. For example x, weight, or total. If we wish to use multiple words, we separate them with underscores. For example first_string or total_of_subtotals.

Functions

We can make a *function*, whose value depends upon some input. We call this input an *argument* – we will be using the word "input" later in the book to mean something different:

```
Python
>>> def cube(x): return x * x * x
...
>>> cube(10)
1000
>>> answer = cube(20)
>>> answer
8000
```

Note that we had to press the Enter key twice when defining the function: we shall discover why momentarily. What are the parts to this definition of the function cube? We write **def**, followed by the function name, its argument in parentheses, and a colon. Then, we calculate x * x * x and use **return** to return the value to us.

We need the word **return** because not all functions return something. For example, this function prints a string given to it twice to the screen, but does not return a value:

```
Python
>>> def print_twice(x):
...     print(x)
...     print(x)
...
>>> print_twice('Ha')
Ha
Ha
>>> print_twice(1)
1
1
```

Notice this function spans multiple lines. It can operate on both strings and numbers. Now you can see why we needed to press Enter twice when defining the cube and print_twice functions – so that Python knows when we have finished entering a multi-line function.

Indentation

Each of the `print(x)` lines in `print_twice` is *indented* (moved to the right by insertion of four spaces). This helps us to show the structure of the program more clearly, and in fact is a requirement – Python will complain if we do not do it:

```
Python
>>> def print_twice(x):
... print(x)
  File "<stdin>", line 2
    print(x)
        ^
IndentationError: expected an indented block
```

You will come across this error frequently as you learn to indent your Python programs correctly.

Functions with choices

We can use the keywords **if** and **else** to build a function which makes a choice based on some test. For example, here is a function which determines if an integer is negative:

```
Python
>>> def neg(x):
...        if x < 0:
...            return True
...        else:
...            return False
```

We can test it like this:

```
Python
>>> neg(1)
False
>>> neg(-1)
True
```

Notice the indentation of each part of this function, after every line which ends with a colon – again, it is required. We can write it using fewer lines, if it will fit:

```
Python
>>> def neg(x):
...        if x < 0: return True
...        else: return False
```

Of course, our function is equivalent to just writing

```
Python
>>> def neg(x):
...        return x < 0
```

because x < 0 will evaluate to the appropriate boolean value on its own – True if $x < 0$ and False otherwise. Here is another function, this time to determine if a given string is a vowel or not:

```Python
>>> def is_vowel(s):
...     return s == 'a' or s == 'e' or s == 'i' or s == 'o' or s == 'u'
>>> is_vowel('x')
False
>>> is_vowel('u')
True
```

If we need to test for more than one condition we can use the **elif** keyword (short for "else if"):

```Python
>>> def sign(x):
>>>     if x < 0: return -1
>>>     elif x == 0: return 0
>>>     else: return 1
```

This function returns the sign of a number, irrespective of its magnitude. Of course, with extra indenting, this could be written without **elif**. Can you see how?

Multiple arguments

There can be more than one argument to a function. For example, here is a function which checks if two numbers add up to ten:

```Python
>>> def add_to_ten(a, b):
...     return a + b == 10
>>> add_to_ten(6, 4)
True
>>> add_to_ten(6, 5)
False
```

The result is a boolean. We use the function in the same way as before, but writing two numbers this time, one for each argument the function expects. Finally, let us use the + operator in a different way, to concatenate strings:

```Python
>>> def welcome(first, last):
...     print('Welcome, ' + first + ' ' + last + '! Enjoy your stay.')
>>> welcome('Richard', 'Smith')
Welcome, Richard Smith! Enjoy your stay.
```

Going round again

A *recursive* function is one which uses itself in its own definition. Consider calculating the factorial of a given number – for example the factorial of 4 (written 4! in mathematics) is $4 \times 3 \times 2 \times 1$. Here is a recursive function to calculate the factorial of a positive number.

```Python
>>> def factorial(a):
...      if a == 1:
...          return 1
...      else:
...          return a * factorial(a - 1)
```

For example:

```Python
>>> factorial(4)
24
>>> factorial(100)
9332621544394415268169923885626670049071596826438162146859296389521759999322991560
8941463976156518286253697920827223758251185210916864000000000000000000000000
```

How does the evaluation of `factorial(4)` proceed?

$$\begin{array}{ll} & \texttt{factorial(4)} \\ \Longrightarrow & \texttt{4 * factorial(3)} \\ \Longrightarrow & \texttt{4 * (3 * factorial(2))} \\ \Longrightarrow & \texttt{4 * (3 * (2 * factorial(1)))} \\ \Longrightarrow & \texttt{4 * (3 * (2 * 1))} \\ \Longrightarrow & \texttt{4 * (3 * 2)} \\ \Longrightarrow & \texttt{4 * 6} \\ \Longrightarrow & \texttt{24} \end{array}$$

For the first three steps, the **else** part of the conditional expression is chosen, because the argument a is greater than one. When the argument is equal to one, we do not use `factorial` again, but just evaluate to 1. The expression built up of all the multiplications is then evaluated until a value is reached: this is the result of the whole evaluation. It is sometimes possible for a recursive function never to finish – what if we try to evaluate `factorial(-1)`?

$$\begin{array}{ll} & \texttt{factorial(-1)} \\ \Longrightarrow & \texttt{-1 * factorial(-2)} \\ \Longrightarrow & \texttt{-1 * (-2 * factorial(-3))} \\ \Longrightarrow & \texttt{-1 * (-2 * (-3 * factorial(-4)))} \\ & \qquad \vdots \qquad \vdots \end{array}$$

The expression keeps expanding, and the recursion keeps going. Helpfully, Python tells us what is going on:

```
Python
>>> factorial(-1)
Traceback (most recent call last):
  File "<stdin>", line 1, in <module>
  File "<stdin>", line 5, in factorial
  File "<stdin>", line 5, in factorial
  File "<stdin>", line 5, in factorial
  [Previous line repeated 995 more times]
  File "<stdin>", line 2, in factorial
RecursionError: maximum recursion depth exceeded in comparison
```

We do not use recursive functions often in Python, preferring the methods of repeated action described in the next chapter. But it can be interesting to think about how they work, and some of the questions at the end of the chapter invite you to do just that.

Almost every program we write will involve functions such as those shown in this chapter, and many larger ones too – using functions to split up a program into small, easily understandable chunks is the basis of good programming.

Common problems

Now that we are writing slightly larger programs which might span multiple lines, new types of mistake are available to us. A common mistake is to forget the colon at the end of a line. For example, here we forget it after an **if**:

```
Python
>>> def neg(x):
...     if x < 0
  File "<stdin>", line 2
    if x < 0
            ^
SyntaxError: invalid syntax
```

Syntax is a word for the arrangement of symbols and words to make a valid program. If we forget the proper indentation, Python complains too:

```
Python
>>> def neg(x):
...     if x < 0:
...     return True
  File "<stdin>", line 3
    return True
    ^
IndentationError: expected an indented block
```

We must also remember to avoid using one of Python's keywords as a variable or function name, even in an otherwise valid program:

```
Python
>>> def class(x): return '30 pupils'
  File "<stdin>", line 1
    def class(x): return '30 pupils'
        ^
SyntaxError: invalid syntax
```

Another common mistake is to omit the **return** in a function:

```
Python
>>> def double(x): x * 2
...
>>> double(5)
>>>
```

In this case, Python accepts the function, and we only discover our mistake when we try to use it.

Summary

We have learned how to give names to our values so as to use and reuse them in different contexts, and to update the values associated with such names. We have written functions whose result depends upon one or more arguments, including multi-line functions. We have seen how to choose a course of action based upon testing the value associated with a name.

Finally, we have experimented with recursive functions to perform repeated processing of one or more arguments. We have explained, though, that recursion is not ordinarily used in Python. In the next chapter, we will introduce the standard Python mechanisms for repeated actions or calculations.

Questions

1. Write a function which multiplies a given number by ten.

2. Write a function which returns `True` if both of its arguments are non-zero, and `False` otherwise.

3. Write a function `volume` which, given the width, height, and depth of a box, calculates its volume. Write another function `volume_ten_deep` which fixes the depth at 10. It should be implemented by using your `volume` function.

4. Write a function `is_consonant` which, given a lower-case letter in the range `'a'...'z'`, determines if it is a consonant.

Optional: playing with recursive functions

5. Can you suggest a way of preventing the non-termination of the `factorial` function in the case of a zero or negative argument?

6. Write a recursive function `sum_nums` which, given a number n, calculates the sum $1 + 2 + 3 + \ldots + n$.

7. Write a recursive function `power(x, n)` which raises x to the power n.

8. Write a recursive function to list the factors of a number. For example, `factors(12)` should print:

```
1
2
3
4
6
12
```

So Far

1 Strings like `'this'`. Printing to the screen with `print`. The numbers ... `-3,-2,-1,0,1,2,3...`. The arithmetic operators `+` `-` `*` and their precedence and associativity. The boolean values `True` and `False` and their operators **and**, **or**, and **not**. Comparison operators `==` `<` `<=` `>=` `>` `!=`. Finding types with `type`.

2 Defining, using, and updating variables with `=`. Defining and using functions of one or more arguments with **def**. Multi-line functions and their indentation. The **return** keyword for returning a value from a function. Conditional statements using **if** and **else** and **elif**. String concatenation with `+`. Recursive functions.

Using Scripts

From now on, instead of showing the actual Python session...

```
Python
>>> def factorial(n):
...     if n == 1:
...         return n
...     else:
...         return n * factorial(n - 1)
```

...we will usually just show the program in a box:

```
def factorial(n):
    if n == 1:
        return n
    else:
        return n * factorial(n - 1)
```

In fact, this is just how Python programs are normally written, in a text file with the `.py` extension, rather than typed directly into Python.

We can use the **from** ... **import** ... construct to access the program from Python. Assuming we have a file `script.py` which looks like the contents of the box above, we can write:

```
Python
>>> from script import factorial
>>> factorial(4)
24
```

We can use **from** ... **import** * to import all definitions from a script. When we have made a change to the file `script.py` in our text editor (and saved the file), Python must be restarted and the script imported anew.

You will notice that, after running the **import** statement, the directory `__pycache__` has appeared alongside `script.py`. This is for Python's internal use, and you may discard it if you like.

Chapter 3

Again and Again

In the previous chapter we used recursion to perform a calculation a variable number of times, and noted its limitations in Python. In this chapter, we learn the ordinary Python way of handling such situations.

A fixed number of times

The **for** ... **in** range(a, b) structure can be used to do something a number of times. For example, to print each of the numbers in the range in turn:

```
for x in range(0, 5):
    print(x)
```

The expressions inside the **for** construct (or loop, as we call it) will be run once for each number in the range. Here is what we see on the screen:

```
0
1
2
3
4
```

We can see that the two arguments to the range function specify where to start, at 0, and where to stop, before 5. And so, the numbers 0 to 4 inclusive are printed. This behaviour is useful when programming, but unintuitive to humans. Let us write a function to print the numbers $1 \ldots n$ as a human might expect:

```
def print_upto(n):
    for x in range(1, n + 1):
        print(x)
```

So now, `print_upto(5)` will print this:

```
1
2
3
4
5
```

What if we want the numbers to be printed all on the same line? The Python `print` function moves to the next line by default. We can suppress this behaviour by supplying an alternative end to the line (`print` usually ends the line with what is called a newline character):

```
def print_upto(n) =
    for x in range(1, n + 1):
        print(x, end=' ')
```

Now the same statement `print_upto(5)` will print the numbers all on one line, with spaces in between:

```
1 2 3 4 5
```

We have used a second argument to the built-in `print` function – it is a named argument, with the name end. Such names help us remember which argument is which.

One inside another

We can, of course, put one **for** loop inside another. Let us write a function to print a times table of any size:

```
def times_table(n):
    for y in range(1, n + 1):
        for x in range(1, n + 1):
            print(x * y, end=' ')
        print('')
```

We have used `print` with the empty string as its argument to move to a new line. Notice how the indentation helps to show the structure of the nested **for** structures. Here is the output of our new function for table size 5:

```
1 2 3 4 5
2 4 6 8 10
3 6 9 12 15
4 8 12 16 20
5 10 15 20 25
```

The columns are not lined up nicely, because some numbers need one digit to print and some need two. We can use the special letter \t, called a tab, to line the letters up (the \ is called the *escape character*, and gives the letter following it special significance.)

```
#Times table of size n, with tabs              # starts a comment
def times_table(n):
    for y in range(1, n + 1):
        for x in range(1, n + 1):
            print(x * y, end='\t')
        print('')
```

Notice we have added a comment (beginning with #) to remind us that this is a different version of `times_table`. You can put as many comments as you like in your programs. Here is the output:

```
1      2      3      4      5
2      4      6      8      10
3      6      9      12     15
4      8      12     16     20
5      10     15     20     25
```

Tabs are a remnant of mechanical typewriter technology, where little metal stops could be placed in certain positions to line up columns at the touch of a button. We can do better by calculating the maximum width of any column, then printing enough spaces after each number:

```
#Times table of size n, with smallest spaces
def times_table(n):
    column_width = len(str(n * n)) + 1
    for y in range(1, n + 1):
        for x in range(1, n + 1):
            print(x * y, end=' ' * (column_width - len(str(x * y))))
        print('')
```

The built-in function `str` converts a number to a string, and the built-in function `len` calculates the length of a string. We also use the * operator to build the string of many spaces from one space. For example, ' ' * 5 is '   '. Here is the output:

```
1  2  3  4  5
2  4  6  8  10
3  6  9  12 15
4  8  12 16 20
5  10 15 20 25
```

Much better.

Ranging over strings

We can also use **for** to loop or *iterate* over things other than ranges of numbers. For example, if we use **for**... **in** with a string, each letter of the string will be selected in turn:

```
def print_spaced(s):
    for x in s:
        print(x, end=' ')
```

The output of `print_spaced('CHARLES')` will be C H A R L E S . In one of the questions you will be asked to find a way to remove that errant last space.

An unknown number of times

What if we do not know how many times to repeat an action until we begin? We can use the **while** construct. For example, let us ask the user for a password before proceeding:

```
entered = ''

while entered != 'please':
    print('Please enter the password')
    entered = input()
```

The built-in `input` function, which has no arguments, allows the user to type in a line of text, returning when the Enter key is pressed. Here is a possible interaction:

```
Please enter the password
no
Please enter the password
password
Please enter the password
please
```

We cannot know how many times we might need to prompt the user for input, and so we could not have done this with a **for** loop. We can build our **while** loop into a function:

```
entered = ''

def ask_for_password():
    while entered != 'please':
        print('Please enter the password')
        entered = input()
```

Notice that our function also has no arguments, just like `input`, and returns nothing. However, it does not work:

```
Python
>>> ask_for_password()
Traceback (most recent call last):
  File "<stdin>", line 1, in <module>
  File "<stdin>", line 2, in ask_for_password
UnboundLocalError: local variable 'entered' referenced before assignment
```

Local and global names

To write this function correctly, we must bring the definition of the `entered` variable inside the function definition – it will be a new, empty, `entered` each time the function is run:

```
def ask_for_password():
    entered = ''
    while entered != 'please':
        print('Please enter the password')
        entered = input()
```

This is called a *local* variable. In our first example, `entered` was a *global* variable. If we really wanted to use a global variable, we would write:

```
entered = ''

def ask_for_password():
    global entered
    while entered != 'please':
        print('Please enter the password')
        entered = input()
```

There is a flaw in this program, however. If we run this version of the `ask_for_password` function twice then, on the second run, the variable `entered` will already have the correct password in it. So it is right that Python warns us of the dangers of global variables by requiring them to be explicitly declared. We will not use **global** in this book again.

Common problems

It is important when building **for** loops to remember `range`, or we may be in for a nasty surprise:

```
Python
>>> for x in (0, 5):
...    print(x)
...
0
5
```

As we have already mentioned, it is important to remember that ranges begin at the first number given and stop before the second number given:

```
Python
>>> for x in range(1, 10):
...    print(x)
...
```

```
1
2
3
4
5
6
7
8
9
```

These are called half-open intervals. They are unintuitive to the beginner, but to the experienced programmer, they are more convenient, making sure that important properties hold. For example, that `len(range(a, b)) == a - b`.

When you begin to write programs with `input`, there is always the chance of problems with unexpected inputs. For example, expecting a number and using the built-in `int` function, which converts a string into a number:

```Python
>>> a = input()
bob
>>> int(a)
Traceback (most recent call last):
  File "<stdin>", line 1, in <module>
ValueError: invalid literal for int() with base 10: 'bob'
```

Later in the book, we will see how to deal cleanly with such situations.

Summary

We have learned about two methods for repeating statements: **for** loops for a known number of times, and **while** loops when we do not know the number of times in advance. We have, along the way, converted from strings and numbers and back again with `str` and `int`, learned how to customize the `print` function, built bigger strings from smaller ones, and calculated the length of a string. We have started to build interactive programs, accepting input from the user.

We now have the tools to build a much wider and more interesting class of programs.

Questions

1. The range construct can be given an extra, third, argument, the *step*. For example range(0, 10, 2) would iterate over 0, 2, 4, 6, and 8. Use this argument to write a function print_down_from which is the same as our print_upto function but prints the numbers in reverse order.

2. Our times table function, even in its final version, can put in too much space. This happens when only the last column contains the longest numbers, for example:

```
Python
>>> times_table(10)
1    2    3    4    5    6    7    8    9    10
2    4    6    8    10   12   14   16   18   20
3    6    9    12   15   18   21   24   27   30
4    8    12   16   20   24   28   32   36   40
5    10   15   20   25   30   35   40   45   50
6    12   18   24   30   36   42   48   54   60
7    14   21   28   35   42   49   56   63   70
8    16   24   32   40   48   56   64   72   80
9    18   27   36   45   54   63   72   81   90
10   20   30   40   50   60   70   80   90   100
```

Here only the final column has a number with three digits. Modify the function to correct this shortcoming.

3. Write a function count_spaces to count the number of spaces in a string.

4. Fix our print_spaced function to remove the errant final space. Hint: remember that the built-in function len can be used to find the length of a string.

5. Write a function which prints a sentence for the user to copy. Have the user type it in, and press Enter. Check if it is correct and print an appropriate message. If it is incorrect, keep going until it is correct.

6. Simplify our password example by supplying the prompt text directly as an argument to the input function. You will need to add the special string '\n', called the newline character, to the end to move to the next line. Simplify it further by finding a way to remove the entered variable. You will need to use the **pass** keyword, which does nothing.

7. Use the input function to write an interactive guessing game. For example, we might see:

```
Python
>>>guessing_game()
Guess a number between 1 and 100
50
Lower!
15
Higher!
40
Lower!
35
Higher
37
Correct! You took 5 guesses.
```

You will need the built-in function `int` which converts a string to an integer. An arbitrary number between 1 and 100 may be obtained in the following way:

```
Python
>>> import random
>>> random.randint(1, 100)
44
```

(Note that we could also use **from** random **import** randint here and write randint instead of random.randint.)

8. Write a function to print a message in Morse code. Here is the table of codes:

A	. –	B	– . . .	C	– . – .	D	– . .
E	.	F	. . – .	G	– – .	H	. . . .
I	. .	J	. – – –	K	– . –	L	. – . .
M	– –	N	– .	O	– – –	P	. – – .
Q	– – . –	R	. – .	S	. . .	T	–
U	. . –	V	. . . –	W	. – –	X	– . . –
Y	– . – –	Z	– – . .	1	. – – – –	2	. . – – –
3	. . . – –	4	. . . . –	5	. . . . .	6	– . . . .
7	– – . . .	8	– – – . .	9	– – – – .	0	– – – – –

There should be three spaces between letters, and seven spaces between words.

So Far

1 Strings like `'this'`. Printing to the screen with `print`. The numbers ... `-3,-2,-1,0,1,2,3`.... The arithmetic operators `+` `-` `*` and their precedence and associativity. The boolean values `True` and `False` and their operators **and**, **or**, and **not**. Comparison operators `==` `<` `<=` `>=` `>` `!=`. Finding types with `type`.

2 Defining, using, and updating variables with `=`. Defining and using functions of one or more arguments with **def**. Multi-line functions and their indentation. The **return** keyword for returning a value from a function. Conditional statements using **if** and **else** and **elif**. String concatenation with +. Recursive functions.

3 Loops of definite duration with **for** ... **in** and `range`. Customizing `print` with the `end` argument. Making a string of number with `str`. Making strings of smaller strings with *. Finding the length of a string with `len`. Loops of indefinite duration with **while**. Accepting keyboard input from the user with `input`. Converting strings to integers with `int`. Global variables with **global**. The empty **pass** statement.

Chapter 4

Making Lists

We have seen simple Python values such as numbers and strings and booleans, but we have not yet seen how to combine them into bigger structures. We do so now.

Introducing lists

A *list* in Python is an ordered sequence of elements. Here is the list containing the words representing the first few numbers:

```
['zero', 'one', 'two', 'three', 'four', 'five']
```

Equally, we could put numbers or booleans in our list, or nothing – the empty list is written []. Here are the first few prime numbers:

```
[2, 3, 5, 7, 11, 13]
```

We can find the length of the list with len, just as we used it to find the length of a string:

```
Python
>>> len([2, 3, 5, 7, 11, 13])
6
```

It is possible to mix up elements of different types:

```
[1, 'one', False]
```

We will not be doing that in this book, however.

Accessing elements

We can fetch a single element from the list (the first element is number 0):

```Python
>>> l = ['zero', 'one', 'two', 'three', 'four', 'five']
>>> l[0]
'zero'
>>> l[5]
'five'
>>> l[6]
Traceback (most recent call last):
  File "<stdin>", line 1, in <module>
IndexError: list index out of range
```

Notice the error when we go out of range. It is uncommon to write large computer programs correctly the first time, and we often have to track down and correct such errors.

Iterating over lists

We can iterate over the elements of a list with a **for** loop, just like we iterated of a range of numbers with range:

```Python
>>> for x in l:
...     print(x + ' has ' + str(len(x)) + ' letters.')
...
zero has 4 letters.
one has 3 letters.
two has 3 letters.
three has 5 letters.
four has 4 letters.
five has 4 letters.
```

There is a connection between this mechanism and the range function we used with **for** loops earlier. We can use the list function to build lists from ranges:

```Python
>>> list(range(1, 10))
[1, 2, 3, 4, 5, 6, 7, 8, 9]
>>> list(range(1, 10, 3))
[1, 4, 7]
```

In fact, we could write a **for** loop by making a list from a range:

```
Python
>>> for x in list(range(1, 5)):
...      print(x)
...
1
2
3
4
```

This has the same effect as simply writing range(1, 5), but needlessly constructs the list of numbers. When we use range on its own no such intermediate list need be created.

Sometimes we need both the index in the list and the item at that index. By using enumerate, and giving two names – one for the index and one for the value – we can do this easily:

```
Python
>>> for i, elt in enumerate([1, 2, 4, 8, 16]):
...      print('2 to the power ' + str(i) + ' is ' + str(elt))
...
2 to the power 0 is 1
2 to the power 1 is 2
2 to the power 2 is 4
2 to the power 3 is 8
2 to the power 4 is 16
```

List slices

We can pick parts of the list out using what is called a *slice*. A slice is defined using start and stop positions:

```
Python
>>> l = ['zero', 'one', 'two', 'three', 'four', 'five']
>>> l[1:4]
['one', 'two', 'three']
>>> l[1:6]
['one', 'two', 'three', 'four', 'five']
>>> l[0:6]
['zero', 'one', 'two', 'three', 'four', 'five']
```

Notice that the stop value defines the position to stop before, just like with a range. We may omit the start or stop value. This will then be taken to stretch to the omitted end of the list:

```
Python
>>> l = ['zero', 'one', 'two', 'three', 'four', 'five']
>>> l[:4]
['zero', 'one', 'two', 'three']
>>> l[1:]
['one', 'two', 'three', 'four', 'five']
```

Even when the slice contains only one value, it is a list of one element, not just the element:

```Python
>>> l = ['zero', 'one', 'two', 'three', 'four', 'five']
>>> l[4:5]
['four']
```

If a slice contains no values, it is the empty list [ ]:

```Python
>>> l = ['zero', 'one', 'two', 'three', 'four', 'five']
>>> l[4:4]
[]
```

A negative number in a slice counts from the end of the list instead:

```Python
>>> l = ['zero', 'one', 'two', 'three', 'four', 'five']
>>> l[-3:-1]
['three', 'four']
```

Adding to a list

We can add an item to the end of a list:

```Python
>>> l = ['zero', 'one', 'two', 'three', 'four', 'five']
>>> l.append('six')
>>> l
['zero', 'one', 'two', 'three', 'four', 'five', 'six']
```

Functions like **append** which are accessed by putting a dot after the value itself, are called *methods*. Notice that the list l is modified, rather than a new list being returned. We can concatenate lists using the same + operator used for concatenating lists and strings.

```Python
>>> l1 = [1, 2, 3]
>>> l2 = [4, 5, 6]
>>> l1 + l2
[1, 2, 3, 4, 5, 6]
```

The lists l1 and l2 are unaltered.

Modifying lists

We have seen that, unlike strings, lists can be modified. Lists are *mutable*, strings *immutable* (from the word mutate, meaning to change). In fact, we can change existing elements as well as adding elements:

```Python
>>> l
['zero', 'one', 'two', 'three', 'four', 'five']
>>> l[0] = 'nought'
>>> l
['nought', 'one', 'two', 'three', 'four', 'five']
```

We can, of course, delete items from the list. We use the built-in **del** construct:

```Python
>>> l = ['zero', 'one', 'two', 'three', 'four', 'five']
>>> del l[1]
>>> l
['zero', 'two', 'three', 'four', 'five']
```

The **del** construct can also be used with a slice:

```Python
>>> l = ['zero', 'one', 'two', 'three', 'four', 'five']
>>> del l[1:3]
>>> l
['zero', 'three', 'four', 'five']
```

Alternatively, if we wish to retrieve an element and delete it too, we can use the pop method:

```Python
>>> l = ['zero', 'one', 'two', 'three', 'four', 'five']
>>> l.pop(1)
>>> 'one'
>>> l
['zero', 'two', 'three', 'four', 'five']
```

The remove method on lists allows us to remove an item by giving not the index but the actual item.

```Python
>>> l = ['zero', 'one', 'two', 'three', 'four', 'five']
>>> l.remove('two')
>>> l
['zero', 'one', 'three', 'four', 'five']
```

If the list contains more than of the given item, only the first is removed. Let us put it back again, in its old position, using the insert method:

```
Python
>>> l
['zero', 'one', 'three', 'four', 'five']
>>> l.insert(2, 'two')
>>> l
['zero', 'one', 'two', 'three', 'four', 'five']
```

Since lists are mutable, we sometimes need to copy a list – simply assigning it to another variable name will not copy it. For this, we can use the copy method:

```
Python
>>> l
['zero', 'one', 'two', 'three', 'four', 'five']
>>> l2 = l
>>> l3 = l.copy()
>>> l[0] = 'nought'
>>> l
['nought', 'one', 'two', 'three', 'four', 'five']
>>> l2
['nought', 'one', 'two', 'three', 'four', 'five']
>>> l3
['zero', 'one', 'two', 'three', 'four', 'five']
```

Membership testing

We can test to see if an item is a member of a list using **in** or **not in**:

```
Python
>>> l
['zero', 'one', 'two', 'three', 'four', 'five']
>>> 'two' in l
True
>>> 'six' not in l
True
```

We can use index to find the index of the first occurrence of a item, so long as it exists:

```
Python
>>> l
['zero', 'one', 'two', 'three', 'four', 'five']
>>> l.index('two')
2
```

Or, we can count the number of occurrence of an item:

```
Python
>>> l
['zero', 'one', 'two', 'three', 'four', 'five']
>>> l.count('zero')
1
>>> l.count('six')
0
```

In the questions we will use many of these mechanisms, as well as exploring some new ones, to build functions which process lists.

Common problems

As soon as we begin to build compound data structures which contain positions, we open ourselves up to getting the positions wrong:

```
Python
>>> l = ['one', 'two', 'three']
>>> l[1]
'two'
```

Equally seriously, we can try to use a position which is simply not available:

```
Python
>>> l[3]
Traceback (most recent call last):
  File "<stdin>", line 1, in <module>
IndexError: list index out of range
```

Often, these errors are exposed only after using a program for a while – we happen to hit a certain input which fails when many others have succeeded. These kinds of errors can be particularly difficult to track down. They occur also when deleting items from the list:

```
Python
>>> del l[3]
Traceback (most recent call last):
  File "<stdin>", line 1, in <module>
IndexError: list assignment index out of range

>>> l.remove('zero')
Traceback (most recent call last):
  File "<stdin>", line 1, in <module>
ValueError: list.remove(x): x not in list
```

And, of course, when looking things up:

```
Python
>>> l.index('zero')
Traceback (most recent call last):
  File "<stdin>", line 1, in <module>
ValueError: 'zero' is not in list
```

In this case, we could check membership in the list first, and use index only if the item is known to be present. Later in the book, we shall learn another way: to let the errors occur, and then to handle and recover from them.

Another problem concerns our use of ranges. A range in Python is not a list:

```
Python
>>> range(1, 10)
range(1, 10)
```

To turn it into a list, we can use list:

```
Python
>>> list(range(1, 10))
[1, 2, 3, 4, 5, 6, 7, 8, 9]
```

For example, we could try to concatenate two ranges:

```
Python
>>> range(1, 10) + range(20, 30)
Traceback (most recent call last):
  File "<stdin>", line 1, in <module>
TypeError: unsupported operand type(s) for +: 'range' and 'range'
```

We must turn them into lists first:

```
Python
>>> list(range(1, 10)) + list(range(20, 30))
[1, 2, 3, 4, 5, 6, 7, 8, 9, 20, 21, 22, 23, 24, 25, 26, 27, 28, 29]
```

This confusion arises because, in the **for** construct, we can use a range without converting it to a list: **for** knows both how to iterate over a range and how to iterate over a list.

Summary

In this chapter we have introduced lists, our first compound data structure. We have manipulated lists by addition and deletion and slicing. We have iterated over lists, and tested items for membership. The range of interesting programs we can write has grown still further. In the next chapter, we will look at some more advanced list functionality.

Questions

1. Write a function `first` to return the first element of a list, and a function `last` to return the last element of the list. You may assume the list is non-empty.

2. Write a function to build a new list which is the reverse of a given list.

3. Write a function to print the minimum and maximum numbers in a list. You may assume the list is non-empty.

4. As well as start and stop positions, a slice may have a third part, the step (just like a step in a `range`). For example `l[0:10:2]`. Write a function `evens` to return a list containing the items at even positions 0, 2, . . . in the given list.

5. A negative step value in a slice selects the elements from end to beginning. Use this to make your `reverse` function simpler.

6. Write a function `setify` which takes a list, possibly containing duplicates, and builds a new list which represents a set with no duplicates. For example, `setify([1, 2, 3, 2, 1])` might yield `[1, 2, 3]` or `[1, 3, 2]`.

7. Write a function `histogram` to print out a table of frequencies of the elements in a list. You might use the `setify` function you have just written to help.

8. The membership tester `in` works on strings too. Use it to write a function which checks if three given words are all in a given sentence.

9. Write a function `copy_list` to copy a list in the same way as the `copy` method, but without using it.

10. Use your `copy_list` function to write a function which removes an item from a list in the manner of the `remove` method, but returns a new list.

11. A *Caesar cipher* is a crude method of making secret messages. The alphabet is 'rotated' by some amount (here, we started at Q instead of A):

    ```
    ABCDEFGHIJKLMNOPQRSTUVWXYZ
    QRSTUVWXYZABCDEFGHIJKLMNOP
    ```

    Each letter in the lower row is the substitute for the letter in the upper row. For example, here is an encoded message:

    ```
    BUII YI CEHU
    ```

    Write a function to generate the rotated alphabet, for any given amount of rotation. Now write encoding and decoding functions for messages.

12. Use lists to improve your answer to the Morse code question from the previous chapter, by using them to hold the code and letter data – rather than using a big **if** construct as before.

13. Randomly generate a secret four digit code (see question 7 of the previous chapter). Have the user repeatedly guess it, telling them how many digits a) were correct and in the correct place; and (b) were correct but in the incorrect place. Repeat until the user gets the right answer.

So Far

1 Strings like 'this'. Printing to the screen with print. The numbers ... -3,-2,-1,0,1,2,3.... The arithmetic operators + - * and their precedence and associativity. The boolean values True and False and their operators **and**, **or**, and **not**. Comparison operators == < <= >= > !=. Finding types with type.

2 Defining, using, and updating variables with =. Defining and using functions of one or more arguments with **def**. Multi-line functions and their indentation. The **return** keyword for returning a value from a function. Conditional statements using **if** and **else** and **elif**. String concatenation with +. Recursive functions.

3 Loops of definite duration with **for** ... **in** and range. Customizing print with the end argument. Making a string of number with str. Making strings of smaller strings with *. Finding the length of a string with len. Loops of indefinite duration with **while**. Accepting keyboard input from the user with input. Converting strings to integers with int. Global variables with **global**. The empty **pass** statement.

4 Lists like $[a, b...]$. The empty list []. Finding the length of a list with len. Retrieving a list item with $l[n]$. Iterating over lists with **for** loops. Iterating with enumerate. Building lists from ranges with list. List slices $l[x:y]$. The append, remove, insert, index, and count methods on list values. Deletion from lists with **del**. Membership testing with **in** and **not in**.

Chapter 5

More with Lists and Strings

We have learned the basics of list manipulation, and practiced them. In this chapter we explore lists further, including their connection to strings. We pick up a few more string methods along the way. Finally we try three advanced list manipulation techniques.

Splitting and joining

We can split a string into a list of its letters, each as a string, using the built-in `list` function:

```
Python
>>> l = list('tumultuous')
>>> l
['t', 'u', 'm', 'u', 'l', 't', 'u', 'o', 'u', 's']
```

We might think the reverse can be achieved using the familiar built-in `str` function, but that just builds a string showing how the list would be printed by Python:

```
Python
>>> str(l)
"['t', 'u', 'm', 'u', 'l', 't', 'u', 'o', 'u', 's']"
```

We could write a function to do it ourselves:

```
def join(l):
    s = ''
    for x in l:
        s = s + x
    return s
```

Here is the result:

```
Python
>>> l = list('tumultuous')
>>> l
['t', 'u', 'm', 'u', 'l', 't', 'u', 'o', 'u', 's']
>>> join(l)
'tumultuous'
```

As you might suspect, there is a built-in join function: it is, somewhat counterintuitively, a method on strings. We specify the empty string and we see this:

```
Python
>>> l = list('tumultuous')
>>> ''.join(l)
'tumultuous'
```

If we specify a different string, it will be used to glue the letters together instead:

```
Python
>>> ' '.join(l)
't u m u l t u o u s'
```

Another method on strings is `split`, which splits a given string into a list of strings, one for each word in the original:

```
Python
>>> s = '   Once   upon a    time   '
>>> s.split()
['Once', 'upon', 'a', 'time']
```

As you can see, multiple spaces are considered the same as a single space, and spaces at the beginning and end are ignored.

Finding strings in other strings

The `find` method gives the index of the first position a string appears in another:

```
Python
>>> s = 'Once upon a time'
>>> s.find('upon')
5
>>> s.find('not there')
-1
```

In one of the questions, you will be asked to write a similar function yourself, from scratch. Of course, we can use indices and slices on strings too:

```
Python
>>> s = 'Once upon a time'
>>> s[0]
>>> 'O'
>>> s[:4]
'Once'
>>> s[:-4]
'Once upon a '
>>> s[-4:]
'time'
```

And so there is no need to convert a string to a list to take advantage of the useful slicing constructs. We can combine these two new techniques to isolate the first sentence in a string by removing anything which follows:

```
Python
>>> s = 'The first sentence. And the second...'
>>> pos = s.find('.')
>>> pos
18
>>> s[:pos + 1]
'The first sentence.'
```

Of course, in practice we would need to check that find does not return -1. What would happen if it did?

Sorting

Now, we leave strings and return to lists. We often need to sort a list into increasing order prior to further processing. This can be achieved with the sort method:

```
Python
>>> l = [1, 2, 3, 2, 1, 3, 2]
>>> l.sort()
>>> l
[1, 1, 2, 2, 2, 3, 3]
```

The list is sorted in-place. The sorted function, on the other hand, returns a new, sorted version of the list, leaving the original list alone.

```
Python
>>> l = [1, 2, 3, 2, 1, 3, 2]
>>> sorted(l)
[1, 1, 2, 2, 2, 3, 3]
>>> l
[1, 2, 3, 2, 1, 3, 2]
```

This is useful when we want to, for example, iterate over a list in sorted order but leave the original data intact for later use.

Two useful functions: map and filter

There are two built-in functions for producing lists by modifying other lists. The first is map which applies a function to each element of a list:

```Python
>>> l = [1, 2, 3, 4, 5]
>>> def square(x): return x * x
...
>>> list(map(square, l))
[1, 4, 9, 16, 25]
```

We must use list to retrieve the result. We shall discuss why in a moment. The second useful function is filter which can be used to select only such elements of a list for which a given function returns True:

```Python
>>> l = [1, 2, 3, 4, 5]
>>> def even(x): return x % 2 == 0
...
>>> list(filter(even, l))
[2, 4]
```

You can imagine how these functions can be used instead of **for** loops, leading to shorter and easier to understand programs. As programmers, we spend a lot of our time reading programs we have already written (or reading programs written by others), compared with the time we spend writing new ones, so such ease of understanding is very important.

Iterators

We have just written this fragment, making use of map:

```Python
>>> l = [1, 2, 3, 4, 5]
>>> def square(x): return x * x
...
>>> list(map(square, l))
[1, 4, 9, 16, 25]
```

Why did we need to use list to convert the result of map into a list? It is because map returns an *iterator* not a list. An iterator is something which can be used to range over a data structure, but does not return a list – it returns items one by one. This means that the individual items are not created until they are needed. We can use a **for** loop over an iterator, without needing to make a list of it:

```Python
>>> l = [1, 2, 3, 4, 5]
>>> def square(x): return x * x
...
```

```
>>> for x in map(square, l):
...     print(x)
...
1
4
9
16
25
```

Another example of a function returning an iterator is Python's `reversed`:

```
Python
>>> reversed([1, 4, 3, 2])
<list_reverseiterator object at 0x7fd45aa03dc0>
>>> list(reversed([1, 4, 3, 2]))
[2, 3, 4, 1]
```

If we use `reversed` in a **for** loop, we would not notice that it did not return a list, but an iterator. Many built-in functions in Python operate over any iterable structure, not just lists: for example, `sum` calculates the sum of any such structure containing numbers.

List comprehensions

Instead of producing one list from another, or producing it manually by repeated use of `append` or `insert`, we can also build a list from scratch using a *list comprehension*. For example:

```
Python
>>> [x * x for x in range(10)]
[0, 1, 4, 9, 16, 25, 36, 49, 64, 81]
>>> [str(x) for x in range(10)]
['0', '1', '2', '3', '4', '5', '6', '7', '8', '9']
>>> [x % 2 == 0 for x in range(10)]
[True, False, True, False, True, False, True, False, True, False]
```

We can also provide a filter inside the list comprehension by adding an **if** at the end. Here are some cubes which are also even:

```
Python
>>> [x * x * x for x in range(20) if (x * x * x) % 2 == 0]
[0, 8, 64, 216, 512, 1000, 1728, 2744, 4096, 5832]
```

Such comprehensions provide a concise and readable way to produce lists of items meeting certain criteria, without having to iterate over them with a **for** loop.

Common problems

The strange formulation of the `join` mechanism, as a method on the string which is being used to glue the other together, can lead to confusion. Consider, for example, the following two strings:

```Python
>>> x = 'marginal'
>>> y = ' '
```

We intend to write the following:

```Python
>>> y.join(x)
'm a r g i n a l'
```

But if we get the strings in the wrong order, the operation still succeeds, but the result is not what we wanted:

```Python
>>> x.join(y)
' '
```

The `find` method on strings has a way of signalling failure which we have not seen before: instead of returning an error, it returns normally but with an answer of -1. We must check for this, otherwise the -1 may be used unwittingly by the rest of the program without errors, for example in a slice:

```Python
>>> 'Once'[-1]
'e'
```

Summary

We have learned about some of the connections between strings and lists, two kinds of ordered data structure. We have manipulated strings by splitting and joining them, and found strings within one another. We have introduced the important topic of sorting. We have seen maps and filters, two powerful mechanisms for processing lists. We have shown how iterators can simplify list-heavy programs. Finally, we have looked at list comprehensions, a way of combining one or more of these mechanisms together.

Questions

1. Use the `sort` method to build a function which returns an alphabetically sorted list of all the words in a given sentence.

2. Use `sorted` to write a similar function.

3. Use a sorting method to make our `histogram` function from question 7 of the previous chapter produce the histogram sorted in alphabetical order.

4. Write a function to remove spaces from the beginning and end of a string representing a sentence by converting the string to a list of its letters, processing it, and converting it back to a single string. You might find the built-in `reverse` method on lists useful, or another list-reversal mechanism.

5. Can you find a simpler way to perform this task, using a built-in method described in this chapter?

6. Write a function `clip` which, given an integer, clips it to the range 1 . . . 10 so that integers bigger than 10 round down to 10, and those smaller than 1 round up to 1. Write another function `clip_list` which uses this first function together with `map` to apply this clipping to a whole list of integers.

7. Write a function to detect if a given string is palindromic (i.e. equals its own reverse). Now use `filter` to write a function which takes a list of strings and returns only those which are palindromic. Then write a function to return a list of the numbers in a given range which are palindromic, for example 1331.

8. Rewrite your `clip_list` example from question 6 in the form of a list comprehension.

9. Similarly, rewrite your palindromic number detector from question 7 in the form of a list comprehension.

So Far

1 Strings like `'this'`. Printing to the screen with `print`. The numbers ... `-3,-2,-1,0,1,2,3`.... The arithmetic operators `+` `-` `*` and their precedence and associativity. The boolean values `True` and `False` and their operators **and**, **or**, and **not**. Comparison operators `==` `<` `<=` `>=` `>` `!=`. Finding types with `type`.

2 Defining, using, and updating variables with `=`. Defining and using functions of one or more arguments with **def**. Multi-line functions and their indentation. The **return** keyword for returning a value from a function. Conditional statements using **if** and **else** and **elif**. String concatenation with `+`. Recursive functions.

3 Loops of definite duration with **for** ... **in** and `range`. Customizing `print` with the `end` argument. Making a string of number with `str`. Making strings of smaller strings with `*`. Finding the length of a string with `len`. Loops of indefinite duration with **while**. Accepting keyboard input from the user with `input`. Converting strings to integers with `int`. Global variables with **global**. The empty **pass** statement.

4 Lists like $[a, b...]$. The empty list `[]`. Finding the length of a list with `len`. Retrieving a list item with `l[n]`. Iterating over lists with **for** loops. Iterating with `enumerate`. Building lists from ranges with `list`. List slices $l[x:y]$. The `append`, `remove`, `insert`, `index`, and `count` methods on list values. Deletion from lists with **del**. Membership testing with **in** and **not in**.

5 Making lists from strings with `list`. The join method `''.join(l)` and the split method `split`. Slices on strings. The `find` method to give the index of one string in another. Sorting lists with `sort` and `sorted`. Making new lists with `map` and `filter`. Lists and iterators. List comprehensions like `[x * x for x in ... if ...]`.

Chapter 6

Prettier Printing

We have been printing out information using the built-in `print` function. Sometimes, however, we have had to concatenate many little strings with + to insert into sentences the values we want to print, or use inconvenient extra parameters like `end=' '` to prevent default behaviour giving an undesirable result. In this chapter, we will review the `print` function, and then explore a better method of printing with Python.

Recalling the print function

The `print` function takes a value. If the value is not a string, it converts it to a string with `str`. Then, it prints it to the screen and moves one line down by printing a newline character:

```Python
>>> print('entrance')
entrance
>>> print(1)
1
>>> print([1, 2, 3])
[1, 2, 3]
```

We have sometimes suppressed the newline by using an `end` argument:

```Python
>>> print('entrance', end='')
entrance>>>
```

Printing with separators

We can supply more or fewer arguments to the `print` function:

```
Python
>>> print()

>>> print('one', 'two', 'three')
one two three
```

We see that `print` with no arguments just prints a newline. Supplying multiple arguments will print them all out, separated by spaces. We can change the separator:

```
Python
>>> print('one', 'two', 'three', sep='-')
one-two-three
```

Easier printing with format strings

The `print` function is useful, but becomes rather clumsy when we are doing more complicated formatting. Python provides more advanced printing through what are called *format strings*. Here is a function to print the minimum and maximum items in a list of numbers as we might write it traditionally:

```
def print_stats(l):
    print(str(min(l)) + ' up to ' + str(max(l)))
```

(We wrote our own minimum and maximum functions earlier, but they are in fact built in to Python). Here it is in use:

```
Python
>>> print_stats([2, 3, 5, 7, 11, 13, 17, 19, 23, 29])
2 up to 29
```

Now, the same function using a format string:

```
def print_stats(l):
    minimum = min(l)
    maximum = max(l)
    print(f'{minimum} up to {maximum}')
```

There are two things to notice. First, the use of `f'` to begin a string instead of just `'`. This denotes a format string. Second, the sections inside the format string which are demarcated with curly braces `{...}`. The variable names in these will be substituted for the values of those variables. In fact, we can put whole expressions in the curly braces, simplifying further:

```
def print_stats(l):
    print(f'{min(l)} up to {max(l)}')
```

Even in this simple example, we can see that it is rather easier to read our program when written with format strings, when compared with the repeated concatenation in the original. Consider a function to print out a table of powers (the ** operator raises a number to a power):

```python
def print_powers(n):
    for x in range(1, n):
        print(f'{x} {x ** 2} {x ** 3} {x ** 4} {x ** 5}')
```

Much like our times table in chapter 3, the columns are not lined up:

```
Python
>>> print_powers()
1 1 1 1 1
2 4 8 16 32
3 9 27 81 243
4 16 64 256 1024
5 25 125 625 3125
6 36 216 1296 7776
7 49 343 2401 16807
8 64 512 4096 32768
9 81 729 6561 59049
```

Format strings can do this for us automatically, with the addition of a *format specifier* within the curly braces. We add :5d at the end of each one. The 5 is for the column width, and d for decimal integer – the number will be right-justified in the column.

```python
def print_powers(n):
    for x in range(1, n):
        print(f'{x:5d} {x ** 2:5d} {x ** 3:5d} {x ** 4:5d} {x ** 5:5d}')
```

Here is the result:

```
Python
>>> print_powers()
1     1     1     1     1
2     4     8    16    32
3     9    27    81   243
4    16    64   256  1024
5    25   125   625  3125
6    36   216  1296  7776
7    49   343  2401 16807
8    64   512  4096 32768
9    81   729  6561 59049
```

Printing to a file

Instead of printing to the screen, we can print to a file by adding a `file` argument to the `print` function:

```python
def print_powers(n):
    f = open('powers.txt', 'w')
    for x in range(1, n):
        print(f'{x:5d} {x ** 2:5d} {x ** 3:5d} {x ** 4:5d} {x ** 5:5d}', file=f)
    f.close()
```

The function open here opens the new file `'powers.txt'` for writing (hence `'w'`). We then supply the `file` argument to the `print` function. Afterward, we must be sure to close the file using the `close` method on the file `f`. A cleaner method is to use the **with** ... **as** structure:

```python
def print_powers(n):
    with open('powers.txt', 'w') as f:
        for x in range(1, n):
            print(f'{x:5d} {x ** 2:5d} {x ** 3:5d} {x ** 4:5d} {x ** 5:5d}',
                  file=f)
```

The file will be closed automatically once the part of the program indented further to the right than the **with** is complete, so there is no need for us to close it explicitly. In the questions, we will use format strings to create some files of our own.

Common problems

We must remember to use the f prefix to our strings when using format strings, or we get the wrong result:

```python
Python
>>> p = 15
>>> q = 12
>>> print('Total is {p + q}')
Total is {p + q}
```

Here is what it should look like:

```python
Python
>>> print(f'Total is {p + q}')
Total is 27
```

Quotation marks can end a format string, even when they are with the {} braces:

```
Python
>>> def two(x): return x + x
...
>>> print(f'Twice is {two('twice')}')
  File "<stdin>", line 1
    print(f'Twice is {two('twice')}')
                          ^
SyntaxError: invalid syntax
```

The solution is to use double quotation marks instead:

```
Python
>>> print(f"Twice is {two('twice')}")
Twice is twicetwice
```

Comments cannot appear inside braces:

```
Python
>>> print(f'This is the result: {result #update later}')
  File "<stdin>", line 1
SyntaxError: f-string expression part cannot include '#'
```

Finally, when opening a new file for output with the **with** ... **as** ... construct, remember that we must specify `'w'`.

```
Python
>>> open('output.txt')
Traceback (most recent call last):
  File "<stdin>", line 1, in <module>
FileNotFoundError: [Errno 2] No such file or directory: 'output.txt'
>>> open('output.txt', 'w')
```

Summary

We have expanded our knowledge of the built-in `print` function beyond the simple uses we encountered before. We learned about the powerful notion of format strings, and how to use them to shorten and simplify our code. Finally we printed to files, so our programs can now have effects persist even when we close Python.

Questions

1. We can print a list like [1, 2, 3] easily using the print function. Imagine, though, that the print function could not work on lists. Write your own print_list function which uses simple print calls to print the individual elements, but adds the square brackets, commas and spaces itself. Do so without using format strings.

2. Now rewrite your function using format strings. Which is easier to read and write?

3. The method rjust on strings will right-justify them to the given width.

   ```Python
   >>> '2'.rjust(5)
   '    2'
   ```

   Use this method to rewrite our print_powers function without format strings, but still with properly lined-up columns.

4. The method zfill on a string, given a number, will pad the string with zeroes to that width. For example, '435'.zfill(8) will produce 00000435. Modify your previous answer to use this function to print our table of powers with uniform column widths padded by zeroes.

5. Write a program which asks the user to type in a list of names, one per line, like Mr James Smith, and writes them to a given file, again one per line, in the form Smith, John, Mr.

6. Rewrite the function from the previous question using format strings, if you did not use them the first time.

7. Use the find function introduced the previous chapter to write a program which prints the positions at which a given word is found in each of given list of sentences. For example, consider this list:

   ```
   ['Three pounds of self-raising flour',
    'Two pounds of plain flour',
    'Six ounces of butter']
   ```

   Your function, given this list and the string 'pound', should print:

   ```
   pound found at position 6 in sentence 1
   pound found at position 4 in sentence 2
   pound not found in sentence 3
   ```

8. Modify your answer to question 7 to print the information to a file with a given name.

So Far

1 Strings like `'this'`. Printing to the screen with `print`. The numbers ... `-3,-2,-1,0,1,2,3....` The arithmetic operators `+` `-` `*` and their precedence and associativity. The boolean values `True` and `False` and their operators **and**, **or**, and **not**. Comparison operators `==` `<` `<=` `>=` `>` `!=`. Finding types with `type`.

2 Defining, using, and updating variables with `=`. Defining and using functions of one or more arguments with **def**. Multi-line functions and their indentation. The **return** keyword for returning a value from a function. Conditional statements using **if** and **else** and **elif**. String concatenation with `+`. Recursive functions.

3 Loops of definite duration with **for** ... **in** and `range`. Customizing `print` with the `end` argument. Making a string of number with `str`. Making strings of smaller strings with `*`. Finding the length of a string with `len`. Loops of indefinite duration with **while**. Accepting keyboard input from the user with `input`. Converting strings to integers with `int`. Global variables with **global**. The empty **pass** statement.

4 Lists like $[a, b...]$. The empty list `[]`. Finding the length of a list with `len`. Retrieving a list item with `l[n]`. Iterating over lists with **for** loops. Iterating with `enumerate`. Building lists from ranges with `list`. List slices `l[x:y]`. The `append`, `remove`, `insert`, `index`, and `count` methods on list values. Deletion from lists with **del**. Membership testing with **in** and **not in**.

5 Making lists from strings with `list`. The `join` method `''.join(l)` and the split method `split`. Slices on strings. The `find` method to give the index of one string in another. Sorting lists with `sort` and `sorted`. Making new lists with `map` and `filter`. Lists and iterators. List comprehensions like `[x * x` **for** `x` **in** `...` **if** `...].`

6 The `print` function with no or multiple values, and the `sep` separator argument. Format strings like `f'Value of a is {a}'`. Writing to files with `open` and `file=` and `close`. Writing to files safely with **with** ... **as**.

Chapter 7

Arranging Things

We have already seen how to combine values into a list. Lists are ordered, and mutable (we may alter elements, or insert or delete them). Sometimes we would like compound values with different properties. In this chapter, we look at three such structures: *tuples*, *dictionaries*, and *sets*. We will see how to choose the appropriate structure for the appropriate task: a program and its data structures are intimately linked.

Tuples

A tuple is a fixed-length collection of values, allowing the whole structure to be given a name and to be passed around just like we pass around any other value. There are two differences with lists: tuples are of fixed length, and their elements may not be altered. Here are some tuples:

```
Python
>>> t = (1, 'one')
>>> t2 = (1, (1, 2), (1, 2, 3))
```

We now have two tuples: the first, t, of length 2, and the second, t2, of length 3, containing within it other tuples. We can take the tuples apart by assigning names. This is called unpacking:

```
Python
>>> a, b = t
>>> a
1
>>> b
'one'
>>> c, d, e = t2
>>> c
1
>>> d
(1, 2)
>>> e
(1, 2, 3)
```

We can pass a tuple to a function as usual, then unpack the values. For example, here is function to add two numbers passed to it as a single tuple of length 2:

```
Python
>>> def f(x):
...      a, b = x
...      return a + b
...
>>> pair = (1, 2)
>>> f(pair)
3
>>> f((1, 2))
3
>>> f(1, 2)
Traceback (most recent call last):
  File "<stdin>", line 1, in <module>
TypeError: f() takes 1 positional argument but 2 were given
```

We can also select items from a tuple using indexing and slicing:

```
Python
>>> t2 = (1, (1, 2), (1, 2, 3))
>>> t2[0]
1
>>> t2[::-1]
((1, 2, 3), (1, 2), 1)
```

Of course, to do this without knowing the length of the tuple might sometimes be difficult. We can use the usual `len` function:

```
Python
>>> t2 = (1, (1, 2), (1, 2, 3))
>>> len(t2)
3
>>> len(t2[1])
2
```

Tuples are immutable – unlike with lists, we cannot change their elements.

```
Python
>>> x = (1, 2)
>>> x[0] = 3
Traceback (most recent call last):
  File "<stdin>", line 1, in <module>
TypeError: 'tuple' object does not support item assignment
```

Of course, if a tuple contains an mutable value such as a list, we can change parts of that inside value:

```
Python
>>> l = [1, 2, 3]
>>> t = (l, l)
>>> l[0] = 4
>>> t
([4, 2, 3], [4, 2, 3])
```

Dictionaries

Many programs make use of a structure known as a *dictionary*. A real dictionary is used for associating definitions with words; we use "dictionary" more generally to mean associating some unique *keys* (like words) with *values* (like definitions). For example, we might like to store the following information about the number of people living in each house in a road:

House	People
1	4
2	2
3	2
4	3
5	1
6	2

We could represent this using a list of pairs represented as tuples. But then we would have to write various functions for looking up or replacing entries ourselves. Python provides a special type for dictionaries, which preserves automatically the property that every key has only one value associated with it. Let us start with an empty dictionary, which is written {}, and add and update some entries:

```
Python
>>> d = {}
>>> d[1] = 4
>>> d
{1: 4}
>>> d[2] = 2
>>> d[3] = 2
>>> d[4] = 3
>>> d[5] = 1
>>> d[6] = 2
>>> d
{1: 4, 2: 2, 3: 2, 4: 3, 5: 1, 6: 2}
>>> d[6] = 8
>>> d
{1: 4, 2: 2, 3: 2, 4: 3, 5: 1, 6: 8}
```

We could, of course, write the whole thing in one go:

```
Python
>>> d = {1: 4, 2: 2, 3: 2, 4: 3, 5: 1, 6: 2}
```

We can see that dictionaries are unordered:

```
Python
>>> {1: 4, 2: 2} == {2: 2, 1: 4}
True
```

Keys in a dictionary must be immutable. For example, we cannot use a list as a key. We can use the usual tests **in** and **not in** to check if a dictionary has a value for a given key:

```
Python
>>> d = {1: 4, 2: 2, 3: 2, 4: 3, 5: 1, 6: 2}
>>> 1 in d
True
>>> 10 in d
False
>>> 10 not in d
True
```

Finally, deletion is performed with the usual **del** statement, providing the key only:

```
Python
>>> d = {1: 4, 2: 2, 3: 2, 4: 3, 5: 1, 6: 2}
>>> del d[2]
>>> d
{1: 4, 3: 2, 4: 3, 5: 1, 6: 2}
```

There is an error if the key is not in the dictionary:

```
>>> del d[7]
Traceback (most recent call last):
  File "<stdin>", line 1, in <module>
KeyError: 7
```

Iterating over dictionaries

How might we iterate over the dictionary entries? We use a **for** loop, but we specify two names: one for the key, and one for the value, and use the items method:

```
Python
>>> for k, v in d.items():
...     print(f'{k} is mapped to {v}')
...
1 is mapped to 4
2 is mapped to 2
3 is mapped to 2
4 is mapped to 3
5 is mapped to 1
6 is mapped to 2
```

Alternatively, we can use an ordinary **for** loop, and simply look the value up:

```Python
>>> for k in d:
...     print(f'{k} is mapped to {d[k]}')
...
1 is mapped to 4
2 is mapped to 2
3 is mapped to 2
4 is mapped to 3
5 is mapped to 1
6 is mapped to 2
```

Should we have key-value pairs already, we can turn a list of them into a dictionary using the dict function:

```Python
>>> dict([(1, 'one'), (2, 'two'), (3, 'three')])
{1: 'one', 2: 'two', 3: 'three'}
>>> dict([(1, 'ONE'), (1, 'one'), (2, 'two'), (3, 'three')])
{1: 'one', 2: 'two', 3: 'three'}
```

Notice that the entry (1, 'ONE') is overwritten, since the entries are added in order.

Sets

In the questions to chapter 4 we wrote a function setify to remove duplicate items from a list. Python has a built-in type for sets: they are just like dictionaries, but with no values.

```Python
>>> s = {1, 2, 3}
>>> s2 = set([1, 2, 3, 2, 1])
>>> s2
{1, 2, 3}
>>> s3 = set('qwertyuiop')
>>> s3
{'w', 'p', 'r', 'e', 'i', 'q', 'o', 'u', 'y', 't'}
>>> empty_set = set()
>>> empty_set
set()
```

Note that the empty set is built by, and printed as set(). This is to distinguish it from the empty dictionary {}. We can use the usual **in** and **not in** tests:

```Python
>>> s = set('qwertyuiop')
>>> 'e' in s
True
>>> 'z' not in s
True
```

To add an item to a set, we use the add method:

```Python
>>> s = set([1, 2, 3, 4, 4, 5])
>>> s
{1, 2, 3, 4, 5}
>>> s.add(7)
>>> s
{1, 2, 3, 4, 5, 7}
```

To remove an item from a set, we use the remove method:

```Python
>>> s = set([1, 2, 3, 4, 4, 5])
>>> s
{1, 2, 3, 4, 5}
>>> s.remove(4)
>>> s
{1, 2, 3, 5}
```

There is an error if the item to remove is not in the set. Finally, there are four operations for manipulating pairs of sets:

Operator	Description
$a \mid b$	items in set a or set b or both
a & b	items in set a and set b
$a \char`^ b$	items in set a or set b but not both
$a - b$	items in set a but not set b

For example:

```Python
>>> a = {1, 2, 3, 4}
>>> b = {1, 2, 5, 6}
>>> a | b
{1, 2, 3, 4, 5, 6}
>>> a & b
{1, 2}
>>> a ^ b
{3, 4, 5, 6}
>>> a - b
{3, 4}
```

Set operations are useful when we need information from two sources to select what to do next, or which data to operate on next.

Common problems

One must take care to distinguish between parentheses used for multiple arguments to a function, and parentheses used for building a tuple:

```Python
>>> def f(a, b): return a + b
...
>>> x = (1, 2)
>>> f(x)
Traceback (most recent call last):
  File "<stdin>", line 1, in <module>
TypeError: f() missing 1 required positional argument: 'b'
```

Tuple unpacking must be explicit. For example, imagine a function we wished to use by passing two arguments, a number and a pair of numbers:

```Python
>>> f(1, (2, 3))
7
```

We might like to write this, but Python will not let us:

```Python
>>> def f(a, (b, c)): return a + b * c
  File "<stdin>", line 1
    def f(a, (b, c)): return a + b * c
             ^
SyntaxError: invalid syntax
```

Instead, we must explicitly unpack the tuple:

```Python
>>> def f(a, pair):
        b, c = pair
        return a + b * c
```

Dictionaries exhibit, of course, the usual lookup errors when a key is not found:

```Python
>>> d = {1 : 2, 2 : 3}
>>> d[3]
Traceback (most recent call last):
  File "<stdin>", line 1, in <module>
KeyError: 3
```

More subtly, it is important to remember that **in** and **not in** refer to the keys present in a dictionary, not the values:

```
Python
>>> d = {1 : 2, 2 : 3}
>>> 3 in d
False
```

Summary

We have looked at some new data structures: tuples for holding two or more items; and dictionaries which assign keys to values. We concluded with sets, which can be used to store information without duplicates, and quickly to test for membership. We have seen how to build sets from strings.

For a long time now, we have been saying that we would address detection and recovery from errors. In the next chapter, we do just that.

Questions

1. We can swap the values of variables a and b by using a temporary variable t:

```Python
>>> a = 1
>>> b = 2
>>> t = a
>>> a = b
>>> b = t
>>> a
2
>>> b
1
```

   Show how to use a tuple to achieve the same result.

2. Write a function unzip which, given a dictionary, returns a pair of lists, the first containing the keys and the second the corresponding values.

3. The opposite function zip, combined with the dict function we have already described, can be used to build a dictionary from two lists: one of all the keys, and one of all the values.

```Python
>>> dict(zip([1, 2], ['one', 'two']))
{1: 'one', 2: 'two'}
```

   Write a function to replace both zip and dict in this circumstance.

4. Write the function union(a, b) which forms the union of two dictionaries. The union of two dictionaries is the dictionary containing all the entries in one or other or both. In the case that a key is contained in both dictionaries, the value in the first should be preferred.

5. The following, flawed function is intended to remove all items equal to zero from a list:

```Python
>>> def remove_zeroes(l):
...     for x in range(0, len(l)):
...         if l[x] == 0: del l[x]
...
>>>
>>> l = [1, 0, 0, 0, 1]
>>> remove_zeroes(l)
Traceback (most recent call last):
  File "<stdin>", line 1, in <module>
  File "<stdin>", line 3, in remove_zeroes
IndexError: list index out of range
>>> l
[1, 0, 1]
```

   Why does it fail? Write a correct version.

6. We can write dictionary comprehensions, much like list comprehensions. For example:

```
Python
>>> {n: n ** 2 for n in range(10)}
{0: 0, 1: 1, 2: 4, 3: 9, 4: 16, 5: 25, 6: 36, 7: 49, 8: 64, 9: 81}
>>> {n: n ** 2 for n in range(10) if n ** 2 % 2 == 0}
{0: 0, 2: 4, 4: 16, 6: 36, 8: 64}
```

Write a dictionary comprehension to 'reverse' a dictionary, that is to make the keys in the original values and the values in the original keys. Why might the new dictionary have a different size from the original?

7. Use sets to write a function which returns the 'letter set' of a list of words. That is to say, the list of all letters used in those words. Now write a function to return a set of all letters not used by them.

8. Imagine Python did not have built-in support for sets. Show how we could use dictionaries to represent sets. Write the four set operations | - ^ & for this new representation of sets.

9. Write the set operation & using set comprehensions. Set comprehensions look a little like the dictionary comprehensions of question 6. We can use two **for** sections to cycle over all pairs of set members i.e. **for** x **in** a **for** y **in** b ...

10. Write a function to add the numbers in a tuple. For example, sum_all(1, (1, 2), 3) should yield 7. You will need to distinguish between integers and tuples by using the test type(x) == int, which is True if the type of x is int.

So Far

1 Strings like 'this'. Printing to the screen with print. The numbers ... -3,-2,-1,0,1,2,3.... The arithmetic operators + - * and their precedence and associativity. The boolean values True and False and their operators **and**, **or**, and **not**. Comparison operators == < <= >= > !=. Finding types with type.

2 Defining, using, and updating variables with =. Defining and using functions of one or more arguments with **def**. Multi-line functions and their indentation. The **return** keyword for returning a value from a function. Conditional statements using **if** and **else** and **elif**. String concatenation with +. Recursive functions.

3 Loops of definite duration with **for** ... **in** and range. Customizing print with the end argument. Making a string of number with str. Making strings of smaller strings with *. Finding the length of a string with len. Loops of indefinite duration with **while**. Accepting keyboard input from the user with input. Converting strings to integers with int. Global variables with **global**. The empty **pass** statement.

4 Lists like [*a*, *b*...]. The empty list []. Finding the length of a list with len. Retrieving a list item with l[*n*]. Iterating over lists with **for** loops. Iterating with enumerate. Building lists from ranges with list. List slices l[*x*:*y*]. The append, remove, insert, index, and count methods on list values. Deletion from lists with **del**. Membership testing with **in** and **not in**.

5 Making lists from strings with list. The join method ''.join(l) and the split method split. Slices on strings. The find method to give the index of one string in another. Sorting lists with sort and sorted. Making new lists with map and filter. Lists and iterators. List comprehensions like [x * x **for** x **in** ... **if** ...].

6 The print function with no or multiple values, and the sep separator argument. Format strings like f'Value of a is {a}'. Writing to files with open and file= and close. Writing to files safely with **with** ... **as**.

7 Tuples, which are fixed-length collections of values (a, b), (a, b, c) etc. Tuple unpacking like a, b = t. Indexing and slicing on tuples, and finding their length. Dictionaries like {}, {k: v}, {k: v, k2: v2} etc. Indexing, adding, deleting, and updating dictionary entries. Looping over dictionaries using the items method. Sets like {1, 2, 3}. Building sets with set and hence the empty set set(). Building sets from strings. The set operators |&^-.

Chapter 8

When Things Go Wrong

As we have seen, sometimes programs fail to produce a result, ending instead in an error. Sometimes, we do not even get that far – Python rejects our program when we type it in, before we have a chance to run it. Sometimes the error is in our program itself, the programmer's fault. Sometimes it is a problem with unexpected input from the user, or the absence of an expected file.

In this chapter, we look at strategies for detecting, coping with, and recovering from these various types of error.

When there is no result

We will begin by looking at Python's mechanism for dealing with null results. You might have noticed that if we forget the **return** keyword, we see this:

```
Python
>>> def f(a, b): a + b
...
>>> f(1, 2)
>>>
```

It looks as if nothing is returned. In fact, the result is a special value called None:

```
Python
>>> f(1, 2) is None
True
>>> None
>>>
```

(We use the **is** operator here instead of ==, for reasons beyond the scope of this book.) Note that None has no printed representation here unless we explicitly use print, or if it appears in a compound structure:

```
Python
>>> print(f(1, 2))
None
>>> def g(a):
...     if a > 0:
...         return a
...     else:
...         pass
...
>>> list(map(g, [-1, 0, 1, 2, 3]))
[None, None, 1, 2, 3]
```

The None value has a type. In fact, it is the only value of that type:

```
Python
>>> type(None)
<class 'NoneType'>
```

Some operations which raise errors have equivalent versions which instead return None on an error. For example, looking up a key in a dictionary with the get method instead of with ordinary indexing returns None:

```
Python
>>> d = {1: 'one', 2: 'two', 3: 'three'}
>>> d[0]
Traceback (most recent call last):
  File "<stdin>", line 1, in <module>
KeyError: 0
>>> d.get(0)
>>> v = d.get(0)
>>> print(v)
None
```

So, we could write a function to look up a list of given keys in a dictionary, returning a list of only the values for which lookup succeeds, and ignoring those for which it fails:

```
def found_values(l, d):
    output = []
    for k in l:
        v = d.get(k)
        if v is not None:
            output.append(v)
    return output
```

(We can write **is not** as well as **is**). For example:

```
Python
>>> found_values([1, 2, 3], {1: 'one', 2: 'two'})
['one', 'two']
```

Exceptions

Python has a mechanism for representing, detecting, and responding to exceptional situations. That mechanism is known as an *exception*. We have just seen an example:

```Python
>>> d = {1: 'one', 2: 'two', 3: 'three'}
>>> d[0]
Traceback (most recent call last):
  File "<stdin>", line 1, in <module>
KeyError: 0
```

The exception here is KeyError, and it carries along with it the number 0 so we know which key could not be found. Let us write a dictionary lookup function which prints our own message and returns -1 if the lookup fails:

```
def safe_lookup(d, k):
    try:
        return d[k]
    except KeyError:
        print(f'Could not find value for key {k}')
        return -1
```

There are two new words here: **try** and **except**. The statements after **try** will be attempted. If they succeed, the function returns as normal. If they fail with KeyError, control transfers to the **except** section. Here is an example failing call:

```Python
>>> safe_lookup({1: 'one', 2: 'two', 3: 'three'}, 0)
Could not find value for key 0
-1
```

By this exception mechanism, we can handle exceptional circumstances without stopping the program, or terminate the program early, but in a controlled manner.

Standard exceptions

Here are some of Python's standard exceptions:

Exception	Description
ZeroDivisionError	Division by zero e.g 1 / (1 - 1)
FileNotFoundError	The given file is not on the computer
EOFError	We have reached the (E)nd (O)f the (F)ile
IndexError	The item or slice is out of bounds e.g [1, 2, 3][4]
KeyError	The specified dictionary key is not found
NameError	The variable was not found
TypeError	A value of the wrong type was given e.g int([1])
ValueError	An invalid value of correct type was given e.g int('fish')

Here is an example of the NameError exception:

```
Python
>>> def add3(x, y): return x + y + z
...
>>> add3(1, 2)
Traceback (most recent call last):
  File "<stdin>", line 1, in <module>
  File "<stdin>", line 1, in add3
NameError: name 'z' is not defined
>>> z = 10
>>> add3(1, 2)
13
```

Notice that z does not have to be defined after the definition of add3 – it may be supplied afterward. This is rather bad practice through, of course.

Raising exceptions ourselves

As well as handling the standard exceptions, we can raise them ourself with the **raise** construct. Here is a function to build a list of repeated elements:

```
def repeated(e, length):
    if length < 0: raise ValueError
    l = []
    for x in range(0, length): l.append(e)
    return l
```

This function raises ValueError if asked to create a list of negative length. For example:

```
Python
>>> repeated(1, 10)
[1, 1, 1, 1, 1, 1, 1, 1, 1, 1]
>>> repeated(1, -10)
Traceback (most recent call last):
  File "<stdin>", line 1, in <module>
  File "<stdin>", line 2, in repeated
ValueError
```

We can give a name to an exception as we catch it, allowing us to use **raise** to *re-raise* the exception:

```
def safe_lookup(d, k):
    try:
        return d[k]
    except KeyError as e:
        print(f'FATAL ERROR: Bad key {k} in dict {d}')
        raise e
```

Here, we have decided that a bad key is a fatal error, but we wish to provide some debugging information including the key and dictionary before the program ends.

Catching any exception

We can catch any exception by using **except** Exception:

```
def safe_lookup(d, k):
    try:
        return d[k]
    except Exception as e:
        print('Unknown error in safe_lookup')
        raise e
```

We would only normally do this to gather up any un-handled exceptions in a large program, and report them cleanly before exiting. Otherwise it is always best to specify which exception we expect to have to handle.

Keeping exceptions small

We should try to keep the part between **try** and **except** as small as possible, so it is clear which statement or statements might fail to complete. We can do this using an optional **else** part:

```
def safe_lookup(d, k):
    try:
        print('attempting key lookup')
        result = d[k]
    except Exception as e:
        print('Unknown error in safe_lookup')
        raise e
    else:
        print('key lookup succeeded')
        return result
```

Notice that the variable result is available in the **else** portion. We can now rewrite, using exceptions, our guessing_game function from the questions to chapter 3. We wish to properly deal with the possibility that the input from the user is either not a number, resulting in a ValueError exception, or that the number is not in range. We will encapsulate this in the new get_guess function, using a fairly benign form of recursion:

```
def get_guess(message):
    try:
        this_guess = int(input(message))
    except ValueError:
        print('Not a number!')
        return get_guess('')
    else:
        if this_guess < 1 or this_guess > 100:
            print('Number not in range 1..100')
            return get_guess('')
        return this_guess
```

We minimise the portion between **try** and **except** by including an **else** section. Now the error handling is confined to the get_guess function, and the main function is relatively simple:

```python
def guessing_game():
    target = random.randint(1, 100)
    guess = get_guess('Guess a number between 1 and 100\n')
    tries = 1
    while guess != target:
        tries += 1
        if guess < target:
            guess = get_guess('Higher!\n')
        elif guess > target:
            guess = get_guess('Lower!\n')
    print(f'Correct! You took {tries} guesses.')
```

Here is the full program:

```python
import random

def get_guess(message):
    try:
        this_guess = int(input(message))
    except ValueError:
        print('Not a number!')
        return get_guess('')
    else:
        if this_guess < 1 or this_guess > 100:
            print('Number not in range 1..100')
            return get_guess('')
        return this_guess

def guessing_game():
    target = random.randint(1, 100)
    guess = get_guess('Guess a number between 1 and 100\n')
    tries = 1
    while guess != target:
        tries += 1
        if guess < target:
            guess = get_guess('Higher!\n')
        elif guess > target:
            guess = get_guess('Lower!\n')
    print(f'Correct! You took {tries} guesses.')
```

Common problems

Being a language which evolved slowly, with no grand design, there is in Python little consistency. Some functions signal error by returning -1, some by returning None, some by raising exceptions. It is important to check the documentation, and make sure to include error handling in our programs at all appropriate points. Even if we have to exit the program on a particularly unusual error (e.g disk full), we can at least print a message. Taking care in this circumstances is crucial to building reliable programs, especially larger ones.

Summary

We have finally addressed the problem of how to deal with errors which occur when running our programs: to detect them, handle them, and recover from them. We have learned about the null result None and how to take advantage of it. We can now add exceptions to our toolbox, choosing between error avoidance and error detection as appropriate in each situation.

In the next chapter, we return to the topic of file processing, writing some more complete programs.

Questions

1. Write a function which, given a list of strings, such as `['1', '10', 'ten', 'tree']` returns their sum, ignoring anything which is not a number made of digits.

2. Rewrite your solution using `map`, `filter`, and `sum`, if you did not use them originally.

3. Use exceptions to write a `safe_division` function which returns 0 if asked to divide by zero.

4. Use exceptions to write a function to prune a dictionary: `dict_take(a, b)` should yield a new dictionary with keys and values drawn from dictionary b, but only if the key exists in dictionary a.

5. Write a function `safe_union` which builds the union of two dictionaries, but raises `KeyError` if there is a clash of keys.

6. Write a function `add_exception` to add value to a set, but which raises `KeyError` if the value already exists in the set.

So Far

1 Strings like 'this'. Printing to the screen with print. The numbers . . . -3,-2,-1,0,1,2,3. . . . The arithmetic operators + - * and their precedence and associativity. The boolean values True and False and their operators **and**, **or**, and **not**. Comparison operators == < <= >= > !=. Finding types with type.

2 Defining, using, and updating variables with =. Defining and using functions of one or more arguments with **def**. Multi-line functions and their indentation. The **return** keyword for returning a value from a function. Conditional statements using **if** and **else** and **elif**. String concatenation with +. Recursive functions.

3 Loops of definite duration with **for** . . . **in** and range. Customizing print with the end argument. Making a string of number with str. Making strings of smaller strings with *. Finding the length of a string with len. Loops of indefinite duration with **while**. Accepting keyboard input from the user with input. Converting strings to integers with int. Global variables with **global**. The empty **pass** statement.

4 Lists like [*a*, *b*. . .]. The empty list []. Finding the length of a list with len. Retrieving a list item with l[*n*]. Iterating over lists with **for** loops. Iterating with enumerate. Building lists from ranges with list. List slices l[*x*:*y*]. The append, remove, insert, index, and count methods on list values. Deletion from lists with **del**. Membership testing with **in** and **not in**.

5 Making lists from strings with list. The join method ''.join(l) and the split method split. Slices on strings. The find method to give the index of one string in another. Sorting lists with sort and sorted. Making new lists with map and filter. Lists and iterators. List comprehensions like [x * x **for** x **in** . . . **if** . . .].

6 The print function with no or multiple values, and the sep separator argument. Format strings like f'Value of a is {a}'. Writing to files with open and file= and close. Writing to files safely with **with** . . . **as**.

7 Tuples, which are fixed-length collections of values (a, b), (a, b, c) etc. Tuple unpacking like a, b = t. Indexing and slicing on tuples, and finding their length. Dictionaries like {}, {k: v}, {k: v, k2: v2} etc. Indexing, adding, deleting, and updating dictionary entries. Looping over dictionaries using the items method. Sets like {1, 2, 3}. Building sets with set and hence the empty set set(). Building sets from strings. The set operators |&^-.

8 The value None denoting the null result and the operator **is** for comparing with it. Handling erroneous situations with exceptions, using **try** . . . **except**. Raising exceptions with **raise**. Minimising the code which might cause an error by using **try** . . . **except** . . . **else**.

Chapter 9

More with Files

In chapter 6, we saw how to print to a file instead of to the screen. In this chapter, we will see how to read information from existing files. Then we will write programs to process data from files, and to edit files.

Reading from files

We shall consider the opening paragraph of Kafka's "Metamorphosis".

```
One morning, when Gregor Samsa woke from troubled dreams, he found
himself transformed in his bed into a horrible vermin.  He lay on
his armour-like back, and if he lifted his head a little he could
see his brown belly, slightly domed and divided by arches into stiff
sections.  The bedding was hardly able to cover it and seemed ready
to slide off any moment.  His many legs, pitifully thin compared
with the size of the rest of him, waved about helplessly as he
looked.
```

There are newline characters at the end of each line, save for the last. You can cut and paste or type this into a text file to try these examples out. Here, it is saved as gregor.txt. Now, we can read the whole contents of the file into a string using 'r' for reading mode:

```Python
>>> f = open('gregor.txt', 'r')
>>> f.read()
'One morning, when Gregor Samsa woke from troubled dreams, he found\nhimself tran
sformed in his bed into a horrible vermin.  He lay on\nhis armour-like back, and
if he lifted his head a little he could\nsee his brown belly, slightly domed and
divided by arches into stiff\nsections.  The bedding was hardly able to cover it
and seemed ready\nto slide off any moment.  His many legs, pitifully thin compare
d\nwith the size of the rest of him, waved about helplessly as he\nlooked.'
>>> f.read()
''
```

This single string contains the \n newline characters, of course. If we call f.read() again, the result is the empty string. This is because there is nothing else left to read – the contents of the file has already been read and we are at the end of the file.

Three ways to iterate over lines

Instead of reading the whole file as one big string, we may read the lines in turn, by repeated use of the readline method:

```Python
>>> f = open('gregor.txt')
>>> f.readline()
'One morning, when Gregor Samsa woke from troubled dreams, he found\n'
>>> f.readline()
'himself transformed in his bed into a horrible vermin.  He lay on\n'
>>> f.readline()
'his armour-like back, and if he lifted his head a little he could\n'
>>> f.readline()
'see his brown belly, slightly domed and divided by arches into stiff\n'
>>> f.readline()
'sections.  The bedding was hardly able to cover it and seemed ready\n'
>>> f.readline()
'to slide off any moment.  His many legs, pitifully thin compared\n'
>>> f.readline()
'with the size of the rest of him, waved about helplessly as he\n'
>>> f.readline()
'looked.'
>>> f.readline()
''
```

Notice that we omit the 'r' argument to the open function – it is the default. Again, we know that there is no more to read when the result is the empty string. We can, alternatively, iterate directly over the contents of the file with a **for** loop:

```Python
>>> f = open('gregor.txt')
>>> for line in f:
...     print(line, end='')
...
One morning, when Gregor Samsa woke from troubled dreams, he found
himself transformed in his bed into a horrible vermin.  He lay on
his armour-like back, and if he lifted his head a little he could
see his brown belly, slightly domed and divided by arches into stiff
sections.  The bedding was hardly able to cover it and seemed ready
to slide off any moment.  His many legs, pitifully thin compared
with the size of the rest of him, waved about helplessly as he
looked.
```

Finally, we can use the list function to return a list of all the lines in the file in one go:

```
Python
>>> f = open('gregor.txt')
>>> list(f)
['One morning, when Gregor Samsa woke from troubled dreams, he found\n', 'himself
 transformed in his bed into a horrible vermin.  He lay on\n', 'his armour-like b
ack, and if he lifted his head a little he could\n', 'see his brown belly, slight
ly domed and divided by arches into stiff\n', 'sections.  The bedding was hardly
able to cover it and seemed ready\n', 'to slide off any moment.  His many legs, p
itifully thin compared\n', 'with the size of the rest of him, waved about helples
sly as he\n', 'looked.\n']
```

Example: reversing lines

We can write a program to read all the lines from a file, and write them in reverse order to another file:

```
Python
>>> f = open('gregor.txt')
>>> f_out = open('output.txt', 'w')
>>> for x in reversed(list(f)):
...     print(x, end='', file=f_out)
...
>>> f.close()
>>> f_out.close()
```

Here is the contents of the output file:

```
looked.
with the size of the rest of him, waved about helplessly as he
to slide off any moment.  His many legs, pitifully thin compared
sections.  The bedding was hardly able to cover it and seemed ready
see his brown belly, slightly domed and divided by arches into stiff
his armour-like back, and if he lifted his head a little he could
himself transformed in his bed into a horrible vermin.  He lay on
One morning, when Gregor Samsa woke from troubled dreams, he found
```

We can use an extended version of the **with** ... **as** structure we have already seen to prevent mistakes with matching up the opening and closing of files. Here is the same program in this simpler, safer, form:

```
Python
>>> with open('gregor.txt') as f, open('output.txt', 'w') as f_out:
...     for x in reversed(list(f)):
...         print(x, end='', file=f_out)
```

Files and exceptions

Not only does the **with** … **as** construct prevent double-closing of a file, but also prevents any attempt
to read from a file which has already been closed:

```Python
>>> f = open('gregor.txt')
>>> f.close()
>>> f.read()
Traceback (most recent call last):
  File "<stdin>", line 1, in <module>
ValueError: I/O operation on closed file.
```

There are still, however, some exceptions we may need to handle, even when using **with** … **as** – for
example, a missing file:

```Python
>>> open('not_there.txt')
Traceback (most recent call last):
  File "<stdin>", line 1, in <module>
FileNotFoundError: [Errno 2] No such file or directory: 'not_there.txt'
```

Example: text statistics

Consider this program to return the number of lines, characters (letters or other symbols), words, and
sentences in a given file:

```
#Text statistics: lines, characters, word, sentences.
def is_full_stop(s):
    return s == '.'

def stats_from_file(f):
    lines = 0
    characters = 0
    words = 0
    sentences = 0
    for line in f:
        lines += 1
        characters += len(line)
        words += len(line.split())
        sentences += len(list(filter(is_full_stop, line)))
    return (lines, characters, words, sentences)

def stats_from_filename(filename):
    with open(filename) as f:
        return stats_from_file(f)

gregor_stats = stats_from_filename('gregor.txt')
```

Notice we can use `filter` directly on `line` without turning it into a list. Here is the result:

```Python
>>> gregor_stats
(8, 472, 85, 4)
```

That is to say, 8 lines, 472 characters, 85 words, and 4 sentences. In the questions, you will be asked to extend this program to collect more statistics.

Common problems

In addition to situations which can lead to file-related exceptions, there are two more common issues which can occur when processing files. If we open a file which already exists, with the intention of writing to it, but we forget to open it in `'w'` mode, an exception occurs:

```Python
>>> with open('exists.txt') as f:
...     print('output', file=f)
...
Traceback (most recent call last):
  File "<stdin>", line 2, in <module>
io.UnsupportedOperation: not writable
```

When printing lines from a file which we have read using, for example, `readlines`, it is important to remember that they will always have a \n newline at the end already. If we print them just using plain `print` we will see double spacing:

```Python
>>> f = open('gregor.txt')
>>> for line in f:
...     print(line)
...
One morning, when Gregor Samsa woke from troubled dreams, he found

himself transformed in his bed into a horrible vermin.  He lay on

his armour-like back, and if he lifted his head a little he could

see his brown belly, slightly domed and divided by arches into stiff

sections.  The bedding was hardly able to cover it and seemed ready

to slide off any moment.  His many legs, pitifully thin compared

with the size of the rest of him, waved about helplessly as he

looked.
```

Summary

We now know how to read from files as well as write to them. This means we can write file-processing programs, which read from one file, process the data in some way, and write to another. This is a significant class of useful programs. We made our programs cleaner and less error-prone by extending our use of the **with** ... **as** construct. We learned how to iterate over the lines in the file, and so over the characters in each line, building our file statistics program. In some of the questions, you will be asked to extend this file statistics program in various ways.

In the next chapter, we fill in another gap in our knowledge: the real numbers – that is to say the ones which are not whole numbers.

Questions

1. We wrote a program to print out the contents of a file line-by-line:

   ```Python
   >>> f = open('gregor.txt')
   >>> for line in f:
   ...     print(line, end='')
   ```

   Rewrite this program using the **with** ... **as** construct.

2. Give a function to write a dictionary with integer keys and string values to a given file. For example, the dictionary {1: 'oak', 2: 'ash', 3: 'lime'} should produce the file:

   ```
   1
   oak
   2
   ash
   3
   lime
   ```

3. Now write a function to read such a dictionary back from file. Make sure to handle exceptions arising from incorrect data. There is a built-in method strip which removes spaces and newlines from either end of a string which may prove useful.

4. When we write to a file which already exists, its contents are overwritten. The file mode 'a' allows information to be appended to a file instead. Use this to write a function which concatenates two files, writing the result to a third.

5. Write a function which reads a file containing multiple numbers, separated by spaces, on multiple lines, and calculates their total.

6. Write a function copy_file which, given two file names, reads the contents of the first, and writes it to the second.

7. Extend our text statistics to print a histogram of the frequencies of each letter in the file. You might remember we wrote a similar histogram program in the questions to chapter 4.

8. Extend it again to print a histogram of frequencies of words. How might punctuation and capital letters be dealt with? Hints:

   - There is a built-in method strip on strings which can be given an argument, a string containing the characters to be stripped.
   - The string string.punctuation following **import** string contains common punctuation characters.
   - The lower method on a string method converts it to lowercase.

9. Write a function to search for a given word in a given file, listing the line numbers and lines at which it appears. Use our lessons from the previous question to deal with punctuation.

10. Write a function top which prints the first five lines from a file, waiting for the user to press Enter for another five, and so on.

So Far

1 Strings like 'this'. Printing to the screen with print. The numbers ... -3, -2, -1, 0, 1, 2, 3, ... The arithmetic operators + - * and their precedence and associativity. The boolean values True and False and their operators **and**, **or**, and **not**. Comparison operators == < <= >= > !=. Finding types with type.

2 Defining, using, and updating variables with =. Defining and using functions of one or more arguments with **def**. Multi-line functions and their indentation. The **return** keyword for returning a value from a function. Conditional statements using **if** and **else** and **elif**. String concatenation with +. Recursive functions.

3 Loops of definite duration with **for** ... **in** and range. Customizing print with the end argument. Making a string of number with str. Making strings of smaller strings with *. Finding the length of a string with len. Loops of indefinite duration with **while**. Accepting keyboard input from the user with input. Converting strings to integers with int. Global variables with **global**. The empty **pass** statement.

4 Lists like [*a*, *b*...]. The empty list []. Finding the length of a list with len. Retrieving a list item with l[*n*]. Iterating over lists with **for** loops. Iterating with enumerate. Building lists from ranges with list. List slices l[*x*:*y*]. The append, remove, insert, index, and count methods on list values. Deletion from lists with **del**. Membership testing with **in** and **not in**.

5 Making lists from strings with list. The join method ''.join(l) and the split method split. Slices on strings. The find method to give the index of one string in another. Sorting lists with sort and sorted. Making new lists with map and filter. Lists and iterators. List comprehensions like [x * x **for** x **in** ... **if** ...].

6 The print function with no or multiple values, and the sep separator argument. Format strings like f'Value of a is {a}'. Writing to files with open and file= and close. Writing to files safely with **with** ... **as**.

7 Tuples, which are fixed-length collections of values (a, b), (a, b, c) etc. Tuple unpacking like a, b = t. Indexing and slicing on tuples, and finding their length. Dictionaries like {}, {k: v}, {k: v, k2: v2} etc. Indexing, adding, deleting, and updating dictionary entries. Looping over dictionaries using the items method. Sets like {1, 2, 3}. Building sets with set and hence the empty set set(). Building sets from strings. The set operators |&^-.

8 The value None denoting the null result and the operator **is** for comparing with it. Handling erroneous situations with exceptions, using **try** ... **except**. Raising exceptions with **raise**. Minimising the code which might cause an error by using **try** ... **except** ... **else**.

9 Opening files for reading in 'r' mode. The read and readline methods. Iterating over a file's lines with **for** or list. Extending **with** ... **as** to open and close multiple files.

Chapter 10

The Other Numbers

The only numbers we have considered until now have been the whole numbers, or integers. For a lot of programming tasks, they are sufficient. And, except for their limited range and the possibility of division by zero, they are easy to understand and use. However, we must now consider the real numbers.

Introducing floating-point numbers

It is clearly not possible to represent all numbers exactly – they might be irrational like π or e and have no finite numerical representation. For most uses, a representation called *floating-point* is suitable, and this is how Python's real numbers are stored. Not all numbers can be represented exactly, but arithmetic operations are very quick.

We can write a floating-point number by including a decimal point somewhere in it. For example 1.6 or 2. or 386.54123. Negative floating-point numbers are preceded by the - character just like negative integers. Here are some floating-point numbers in Python:

```Python
>>> type(1.5)
<class 'float'>
>>> 6.
6.0
>>> -2.3456
-2.3456
>>> 1.0 + 2.5 * 3.0
8.5
>>> 1.0 / 1000.0
0.001
```

Mixing different kinds of number

When we mix integers and floating-point numbers, Python will automatically convert the integer to a floating point so that the operation can work:

```
Python
>>> 1 + 2 * 3.0
7.0
```

Here the integer 2 is converted to the floating-point number 2.0 for the multiplication, which results in the floating-point result 6.0. Then the integer 1 must be similarly converted to a floating-point number to do the addition and produce the final result. The conversion only happens when the expression requires it:

```
Python
>>> type(1 + 2)
<class 'int'>
>>> type(1 + 2.0)
<class 'float'>
```

Sometimes an operation on two integers can produce a floating-point result, for example using the division operator:

```
Python
>>> 1 / 2
0.5
```

You can see now why we introduced addition, subtraction, and multiplication in chapter 1, but left out division. There is an integer division operator too:

```
Python
>>> 2 // 3
0
>>> 10 // 5
2
```

You can see that this operator calculates just the whole part. We already have the % modulus operator to calculate the remainder.

Limits of range and precision

Here is an example of the limits of precision in floating-point operations:

```
Python
>>> 3.123 - 3.0
0.12300000000000022
```

Very small or very large numbers are written using so-called scientific notation:

```Python
>>> 1.0 / 100000.0
1e-05
>>> 30000. ** 10.
5.9049e+44
```

These are the numbers 1×10^{-5} and 5.9049×10^{44} respectively. We can find out the range of numbers available:

```Python
>>> import sys
>>> sys.float_info.max
1.7976931348623157e+308
>>> sys.float_info.min
2.2250738585072014e-308
```

Working with floating-point numbers requires care, and a comprehensive discussion is outside the scope of this book. These challenges exist in any programming language using the floating-point system. We will leave these complications for now – just be aware that they are lurking and must be confronted when writing robust numerical programs.

Standard functions

There are two built-in functions for converting between integers and floating-point numbers:

Function	Description
float	Convert an integer to a floating-point number.
int	Build an integer from a floating-point number, ignoring the non-integer part.

Notice that int is not the expected rounding function:

```Python
>>> float(2)
2.0
>>> int(2.3)
2
>>> int(2.8)
2
```

If we use **import** math, more functions are available:

Function	Description
sqrt	Square root of a number.
log	Natural logarithm.
log10	Logarithm base ten.
sin	Sine of an angle, given in radians.
cos	Cosine of an angle, given in radians.
tan	Tangent of an angle, given in radians.
atan	Arctangent of an angle, given in radians.
ceil	Calculate the nearest whole number at least as big as a floating-point number.
floor	The nearest whole number at least as small as a floating-point number.

For example, we can calculate:

```Python
>>> import math
>>> math.sqrt(3 * 3 + 4 * 4)
5.0
>>> math.sqrt(2)
1.4142135623730951
```

The ceiling and floor functions give us the rounding behaviour we expect:

```Python
>>> math.ceil(2.3)
3
>>> math.floor(2.3)
2
>>> math.ceil(2.5)
3
```

Note that they return integers. But we can get back to floating-point easily, of course:

```Python
>>> float(math.ceil(2.7))
3.0
```

Example: vectors

Let us write some functions with floating-point numbers. We will write some simple operations on vectors in two dimensions. We will represent a point as a pair of floating-point numbers such as (2.0, 3.0). We will represent a vector as a pair of floating-point numbers too. Now we can write a function to build a vector from one point to another, one to find the length of a vector, one to offset a point by a vector, and one to scale a vector to a given length:

```
import math

def make_vector(a, b):
    x0, y0 = a
    x1, y1 = b
    return (x1 - x0, y1 - y0)

def vector_length(v):
    x, y = v
    return math.sqrt(x * x + y * y)

def offset_point(pt, off):
    x, y = pt
    px, py = off
    return (px + x, py + y)

def scale_to_length(l, v):
    currentlength = vector_length(v)
    if currentlength == 0.0:
        return v
    else:
        factor = l / currentlength
        x, y = v
        return (x * factor, y * factor)
```

Notice that we have to be careful about division by zero, just as with integers. We have used tuples for the points because it is easier to read this way – we could have passed each floating-point number as a separate argument instead, of course.

Floating-point numbers are often essential, but must be used with caution. You will discover this when answering the questions for this chapter. Some of these questions require using the built-in functions listed in the table above.

Common problems

We should never use floating-point numbers to represent currency. For example, selling 145 items at $2.34:

```
Python
>>> 145 * 2.34
339.29999999999995
```

Instead, we can store the numbers as integer amounts of cents:

```
Python
>>> 145 * 234
33930
```

We only need consider dollars when formatting the number for printing, not when calculating with it.

Repeated calculations can lead to errors compounding. For example, repeated addition is not the same as multiplication when it comes to floating-point numbers:

```Python
>>> x = 0.0
>>> for y in range(10):
...     x += 0.1
...
>>> x
0.9999999999999999
>>> 0.1 * 10
1.0
```

Summary

We have filled in a gap in our knowledge of Python: how to use real numbers, or floating-point approximations of them. We have learned to be wary of them, and so to use them only when really needed. We looked at the wide range of standard functions for manipulating floating-point numbers, including the `floor` and `ceil` functions, and the `int` and `float` functions for converting between floating point numbers and integers.

In the next chapter we look at the Python Standard Library, Python's collection of helpful modules, in more depth.

Questions

1. Give a function which rounds a positive floating-point number to the nearest whole number, returning another floating-point number.

2. Write a function to find the point equidistant from two given points in two dimensions.

3. Write a function to separate a floating-point number into its whole and fractional parts. Return them as a tuple.

4. Write a function `star` which, given a floating-point number between zero and one, draws an asterisk to indicate the position. An argument of zero will result in an asterisk in column one, and an argument of one an asterisk in column fifty.

5. Now write a function `plot` which, given a function which takes and returns a real number, a start and end point, and a step size, uses `star` to draw a graph. For example we might see:

```
>>> plot (math.sin, 0, math.pi, math.pi / 20)
*
        *
              *
                 *
                    *
                       *
                          *
                             *
                               *
                                 *
                                   *
                                   *
                                   *
                                 *
                               *
                            *
                         *
                      *
                  *
              *
          *
      *
  *
*
```

Here, we have plotted the sine function on the range $0 \ldots \pi$ in steps of size $\pi/20$.

So Far

1 Strings like `'this'`. Printing to the screen with `print`. The numbers ... `-3,-2,-1,0,1,2,3`.... The arithmetic operators `+` `-` `*` and their precedence and associativity. The boolean values `True` and `False` and their operators **and**, **or**, and **not**. Comparison operators `==` `<` `<=` `>=` `>` `!=`. Finding types with `type`.

2 Defining, using, and updating variables with `=`. Defining and using functions of one or more arguments with **def**. Multi-line functions and their indentation. The **return** keyword for returning a value from a function. Conditional statements using **if** and **else** and **elif**. String concatenation with `+`. Recursive functions.

3 Loops of definite duration with **for** ... **in** and `range`. Customizing `print` with the end argument. Making a string of number with `str`. Making strings of smaller strings with `*`. Finding the length of a string with `len`. Loops of indefinite duration with **while**. Accepting keyboard input from the user with `input`. Converting strings to integers with `int`. Global variables with **global**. The empty **pass** statement.

4 Lists like $[a, b...]$. The empty list `[]`. Finding the length of a list with `len`. Retrieving a list item with $l[n]$. Iterating over lists with **for** loops. Iterating with `enumerate`. Building lists from ranges with `list`. List slices $l[x:y]$. The `append`, `remove`, `insert`, `index`, and `count` methods on list values. Deletion from lists with **del**. Membership testing with **in** and **not in**.

5 Making lists from strings with `list`. The join method `''.join(l)` and the split method `split`. Slices on strings. The `find` method to give the index of one string in another. Sorting lists with `sort` and `sorted`. Making new lists with `map` and `filter`. Lists and iterators. List comprehensions like `[x * x for x in ... if ...]`.

6 The `print` function with no or multiple values, and the `sep` separator argument. Format strings like `f'Value of a is {a}'`. Writing to files with `open` and `file=` and `close`. Writing to files safely with **with** ... **as**.

7 Tuples, which are fixed-length collections of values `(a, b)`, `(a, b, c)` etc. Tuple unpacking like `a, b = t`. Indexing and slicing on tuples, and finding their length. Dictionaries like `{}`, `{k: v}`, `{k: v, k2: v2}` etc. Indexing, adding, deleting, and updating dictionary entries. Looping over dictionaries using the `items` method. Sets like `{1, 2, 3}`. Building sets with `set` and hence the empty set `set()`. Building sets from strings. The set operators `|&^-`.

8 The value `None` denoting the null result and the operator **is** for comparing with it. Handling erroneous situations with exceptions, using **try** ... **except**. Raising exceptions with **raise**. Minimising the code which might cause an error by using **try** ... **except** ... **else**.

9 Opening files for reading in `'r'` mode. The `read` and `readline` methods. Iterating over a file's lines with **for** or `list`. Extending **with** ... **as** to open and close multiple files.

10 Floating-point numbers, such as `1.5`, `4e20`, and so on. The division operator `/`. Converting between floating-point numbers and integers with `int` and `float`. The functions on floating-point numbers `math.sqrt`, `math.log`, `math.sin` etc. The floor and ceiling functions `math.floor` and `math.ceil`.

Chapter 11

The Standard Library

We can divide the words and symbols we have been using to build Python programs into three kinds:

1. The language itself. For example, words like **if** and **return**. These also include operators like +.

2. Things which are not part of the language, but which are always available, such as input and map.

3. Things we had to ask for specifically by using **import**. These are extra modules supplied with Python, and called the Standard Library.

It is this last category which concerns us here.

Python's Standard Library

The Python Standard library is divided into modules, one for each area of functionality (in the next chapter, we will learn how to write our own modules). We have already seen how to use **import** statement to make available functions from a module. Here are the modules we have already used from the Standard Library:

Math	Mathematical functions, especially for floating-point numbers.
String	Common string operations and string constants.
Random	Random number and value generation.
Sys	System configuration information and command line arguments.

More about importing modules

On page 21, we introduced the **import** construct. Let us review it now. We can use **from ... import ...** to access definitions and functions from another module. As we know, the functions from a module can be used by putting a period (full stop) between the module name and the function. As an example, the perm function in the math module can be used like this:

```
Python
>>> import math
>>> math.perm(5, 2)
20
```

We can use **from** ... **import** * to import all definitions from a script:

```
Python
>>> from math import *
>>> perm(5, 2)
20
```

We would not normally do this with Standard Library modules: names may clash with our own functions, leading to bugs. We can reduce this problem by importing only the functions we want:

```
Python
>>> from math import perm, factorial
>>> perm(5, 2)
20
>>> factorial(10)
3628800
>>> ceil(2.3)
Traceback (most recent call last):
  File "<stdin>", line 1, in <module>
NameError: name 'ceil' is not defined
```

In any event, if we need to use a function with a long name several times, we can rename it ourselves:

```
Python
>>> import math
>>> fac = math.factorial
>>> fac(10)
3628800
```

Example: the math module

We will take the math module as an example. You can find the documentation for the Python Standard Library installed with your copy of Python, or on the internet. Make sure you are looking at the documentation for Python 3, not any earlier version. Here is the Python documentation for math.perm:

---

math.**perm**(*n*, *k=None*)

Return the number of ways to choose *k* items from *n* items without repetition and with order.

Evaluates to n! / (n - k)! when k <= n and evaluates to zero when k > n.

If *k* is not specified or is None, then *k* defaults to *n* and the function returns n!.

Raises TypeError if either of the arguments are not integers. Raises ValueError if either of the arguments are negative.

New in version 3.8.

In the documentation, we are told what the function does for each argument, and what exceptions may be raised.

Summary

We have learned how to look up functions in the documentation for Python's Standard Library, giving us access to a huge range of modules for everything from text processing, to graphics, to internet programming. In the next chapter, we will talk more about structuring the sort of larger programs we might write using a combination of our own functions and Standard Library functions.

The questions for this chapter use functions from the Standard Library, so you will need to have a copy of the documentation to hand.

Questions

1. Compare the `math.factorial` function supplied with Python to the one we wrote in chapter 2. How do they differ?

2. Use the `string` module to write a function which detects if a given string represents a positive integer or not.

3. The function `getpass.getpass` from the `getpass` module can be used to accept input from the user without showing it on screen, in the manner in which we might type a password. Use this function to write a version of the guessing game from chapter 3 question 7 which allows one person to set up the guessing game in front of another, choosing the number to be guessed.

4. Use the `statistics` module to calculate the median, mode, and mean of a given list of numbers.

5. Use the functions `time.time` and `time.sleep` from the `time` module to write a reaction-time testing game.

So Far

1 Strings like `'this'`. Printing to the screen with `print`. The numbers ... `-3,-2,-1,0,1,2,3`.... The arithmetic operators `+` `-` `*` and their precedence and associativity. The boolean values `True` and `False` and their operators **and**, **or**, and **not**. Comparison operators `== < <= >= > !=`. Finding types with `type`.

2 Defining, using, and updating variables with `=`. Defining and using functions of one or more arguments with **def**. Multi-line functions and their indentation. The **return** keyword for returning a value from a function. Conditional statements using **if** and **else** and **elif**. String concatenation with `+`. Recursive functions.

3 Loops of definite duration with **for** ... **in** and `range`. Customizing `print` with the end argument. Making a string of number with `str`. Making strings of smaller strings with `*`. Finding the length of a string with `len`. Loops of indefinite duration with **while**. Accepting keyboard input from the user with `input`. Converting strings to integers with `int`. Global variables with **global**. The empty **pass** statement.

4 Lists like $[a, b...]$. The empty list `[]`. Finding the length of a list with `len`. Retrieving a list item with $l[n]$. Iterating over lists with **for** loops. Iterating with `enumerate`. Building lists from ranges with `list`. List slices $l[x:y]$. The `append`, `remove`, `insert`, `index`, and `count` methods on list values. Deletion from lists with **del**. Membership testing with **in** and **not in**.

5 Making lists from strings with `list`. The join method `''.join(l)` and the split method `split`. Slices on strings. The `find` method to give the index of one string in another. Sorting lists with `sort` and `sorted`. Making new lists with `map` and `filter`. Lists and iterators. List comprehensions like `[x * x for x in ... if ...]`.

6 The `print` function with no or multiple values, and the `sep` separator argument. Format strings like `f'Value of a is {a}'`. Writing to files with `open` and `file=` and `close`. Writing to files safely with **with** ... **as**.

7 Tuples, which are fixed-length collections of values `(a, b)`, `(a, b, c)` etc. Tuple unpacking like `a, b = t`. Indexing and slicing on tuples, and finding their length. Dictionaries like `{}`, `{k: v}`, `{k: v, k2: v2}` etc. Indexing, adding, deleting, and updating dictionary entries. Looping over dictionaries using the `items` method. Sets like `{1, 2, 3}`. Building sets with `set` and hence the empty set `set()`. Building sets from strings. The set operators `| & ^ -`.

8 The value `None` denoting the null result and the operator **is** for comparing with it. Handling erroneous situations with exceptions, using **try** ... **except**. Raising exceptions with **raise**. Minimising the code which might cause an error by using **try** ... **except** ... **else**.

9 Opening files for reading in `'r'` mode. The `read` and `readline` methods. Iterating over a file's lines with **for** or `list`. Extending **with** ... **as** to open and close multiple files.

10 Floating-point numbers, such as `1.5`, `4e20`, and so on. The division operator `/`. Converting between floating-point numbers and integers with `int` and `float`. The functions on floating-point numbers `math.sqrt`, `math.log`, `math.sin` etc. The floor and ceiling functions `math.floor` and `math.ceil`.

11 Finding the documentation for, and making use of, functions from the Python Standard Library.

Chapter 12

Building Bigger Programs

We have been building progressively larger and larger programs, but they have all been run from Python's interactive interpreter. Now, we shall write stand-alone programs, to be invoked at the command line. This means we can use them just like any other program on our computer, or share them with friends.

Stand-alone programs

We wish to build stand-alone programs which we can run directly from the command line. The `sys` module provides the list `sys.argv` which contains, first, the name of the running script, and then any other arguments provided when the script was run. For example, consider the following program, saved as `standalone.py`:

```
import sys

print(f'This progam is called {sys.argv[0]}')

print(f'There are {len(sys.argv) - 1} command line arguments')

for n, arg in enumerate(sys.argv[1:]):
  print(f'Argument {n} is {arg}')
```

We can run it and see what happens:

```
$ python standalone.py
This program is called standalone.py
There are 0 command line arguments
$ python standalone.py a b c
This program is called standalone.py
There are 3 command line arguments
Argument 0 is a
```

```
Argument 1 is b
Argument 2 is c
```

Remember that on some systems, you might need to type python3 instead of python. The $ is the command line prompt on the author's computer – it may be different on yours.

Now we can write stand-alone programs, to which we provide filenames and other arguments, instead of putting those details directly in the Python program itself. Much more flexible!

A stand-alone text statistics program

We shall now write a stand-alone version of out text statistics program from chapter 9. It will take the filename as an argument. In addition, we shall split our program into two: a file textstat.py to contain the bulk of the program, and another textstats.py to contain the part to do with command line arguments. Here is textstat.py:

```python
#Text statistics: lines, characters, words, and sentences.
def is_full_stop(s):
    return s == '.'

def stats_from_file(f):
    lines = 0
    characters = 0
    words = 0
    sentences = 0
    for line in f:
        lines += 1
        characters += len(line)
        words += len(line.split())
        sentences += len(list(filter(is_full_stop, line)))
    return (lines, characters, words, sentences)

def stats_from_filename(filename):
    with open(filename) as f:
        return stats_from_file(f)
```

Now, we can write the main program textstats.py, which will use the **import** keyword to access the stats_from_filename function of the textstat module.

```python
import sys
import textstat

if len(sys.argv) > 1:
    ls, cs, ws, ss = textstat.stats_from_filename(sys.argv[1])
    print(f'{ls} lines, {cs} characters, {ws} words, {ss} sentences')
```

The purpose of splitting the program this way is to allow the function `stats_from_file` and the function `stats_from_filename` to be used in other contexts without having to alter the whole program. Now we can run the program on its own, without loading an interactive Python session:

```
$ python textstats.py gregor.txt
8 lines, 472 characters, 85 words, 4 sentences
```

In the questions, we will make stand-alone versions of some of our other programs, and some entirely new ones.

Common problems

It is important, just as with any other list, to check that there is as much information as we expect in `sys.argv`, before looking up elements in it, or slicing it. If not, we can print out an error message, and a description of correct usage for the user. For example:

```python
import sys
import textstat

if len(sys.argv) > 1:
    ls, cs, ws, ss = textstat.stats_from_filename(sys.argv[1])
    print(f'{ls} lines, {cs} characters, {ws} words, {ss} sentences')
else:
    print('Bad command line.')
    print('    textstats.py expects one argument, the file name.')
```

Summary

We have gone all the way from introducing addition in chapter 1, to building stand-alone programs in this chapter. We now have the tools to tackle larger projects, and that is what we shall be doing in the next four chapters.

Questions

1. In question 3 of chapter 11 we updated our number-guessing game. Make a stand-alone program from this. It should take one argument, which is the maximum number. If no number is given, 100 is used as a default.

2. In question 5 of chapter 10 we wrote a function to plot a graph of a given function. Write a self-contained command line program to plot any function given as an argument, over a range similarly given. The built-in Python function `eval` can evaluate a given piece of Python program. For example, if the variable x has value `10` the result of `eval('x * 2')` is `20`. Be sure to split your program into two modules: one to deal with the command line argument and one to do the graph plotting. Handle errors appropriately.

3. Write a simple note-taking program. When we run `python note.py add todo "mow the lawn"` the note `mow the lawn` should be added to the end of the file `todo.txt`. If the file does not exist, it should be created. Now extend the program to allow `python note.py list` which will list the notes by number. Running `python note.py remove 4` should remove task number 4.

So Far

1 Strings like `'this'`. Printing to the screen with `print`. The numbers ... `-3,-2,-1,0,1,2,3`.... The arithmetic operators `+` `-` `*` and their precedence and associativity. The boolean values `True` and `False` and their operators **and**, **or**, and **not**. Comparison operators `==` `<` `<=` `>=` `>` `!=`. Finding types with `type`.

2 Defining, using, and updating variables with `=`. Defining and using functions of one or more arguments with **def**. Multi-line functions and their indentation. The **return** keyword for returning a value from a function. Conditional statements using **if** and **else** and **elif**. String concatenation with `+`. Recursive functions.

3 Loops of definite duration with **for** ... **in** and `range`. Customizing `print` with the `end` argument. Making a string of number with `str`. Making strings of smaller strings with `*`. Finding the length of a string with `len`. Loops of indefinite duration with **while**. Accepting keyboard input from the user with `input`. Converting strings to integers with `int`. Global variables with **global**. The empty **pass** statement.

4 Lists like $[a, b...]$. The empty list `[]`. Finding the length of a list with `len`. Retrieving a list item with $l[n]$. Iterating over lists with **for** loops. Iterating with `enumerate`. Building lists from ranges with `list`. List slices $l[x:y]$. The `append`, `remove`, `insert`, `index`, and `count` methods on list values. Deletion from lists with **del**. Membership testing with **in** and **not in**.

5 Making lists from strings with `list`. The `join` method `''.join(l)` and the split method `split`. Slices on strings. The `find` method to give the index of one string in another. Sorting lists with `sort` and `sorted`. Making new lists with `map` and `filter`. Lists and iterators. List comprehensions like `[x * x `**for**` x `**in**` ... `**if**` ...]`.

6 The `print` function with no or multiple values, and the `sep` separator argument. Format strings like `f'Value of a is {a}'`. Writing to files with `open` and `file=` and `close`. Writing to files safely with **with** ... **as**.

7 Tuples, which are fixed-length collections of values `(a, b)`, `(a, b, c)` etc. Tuple unpacking like `a, b = t`. Indexing and slicing on tuples, and finding their length. Dictionaries like `{}`, `{k: v}`, `{k: v, k2: v2}` etc. Indexing, adding, deleting, and updating dictionary entries. Looping over dictionaries using the `items` method. Sets like `{1, 2, 3}`. Building sets with `set` and hence the empty set `set()`. Building sets from strings. The set operators `|&ˆ-`.

8 The value `None` denoting the null result and the operator **is** for comparing with it. Handling erroneous situations with exceptions, using **try** ... **except**. Raising exceptions with **raise**. Minimising the code which might cause an error by using **try** ... **except** ... **else**.

9 Opening files for reading in `'r'` mode. The `read` and `readline` methods. Iterating over a file's lines with **for** or `list`. Extending **with** ... **as** to open and close multiple files.

10 Floating-point numbers, such as `1.5`, `4e20`, and so on. The division operator `/`. Converting between floating-point numbers and integers with `int` and `float`. The functions on floating-point numbers `math.sqrt`, `math.log`, `math.sin` etc. The floor and ceiling functions `math.floor` and `math.ceil`.

11 Finding the documentation for, and making use of, functions from the Python Standard Library.

12 The command line argument list `sys.argv`. Splitting our programs into multiple `.py` files for clarity. Building stand-alone programs we can run from the command line.

Project 1: Pretty Pictures

So far we have been concerned only with programs which read and write text. But we have been sitting in front of a computer with graphical elements on the screen as well as textual ones.

There are many ways to produce pictures, both line drawing and photographic, using programming languages like Python. For this project, we will use the turtle module which uses a model of drawing invented for children but fun for adults too. In this model, there is a little 'turtle' on screen, and we direct it where to go, and it leaves a trail behind it as it goes.

To begin, we import the turtle module, and create a new turtle, which we call t:

```
Python
>>> import turtle
>>> t = turtle.Turtle()
```

Upon typing the second line, a blank window appears, with the turtle represented by an arrow, pointing to the right:

We can now issue a command for the turtle to follow:

```Python
>>> t.forward(100)
```

Here is the result:

We can complete the square by turning repeatedly by ninety degrees and moving forward.

```Python
>>> t.right(90)
>>> t.forward(100)
>>> t.right(90)
>>> t.forward(100)
>>> t.right(90)
>>> t.forward(100)
```

The final result is a square of side 100, with the turtle in its original position, but pointing upwards:

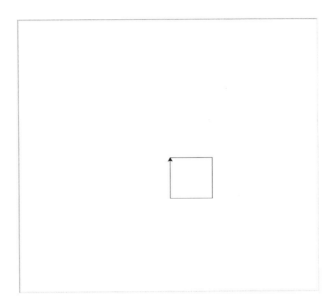

We can write a function to make a square of any size:

```Python
>>> def square(x):
...     for _ in range(4):
...         t.fd(x)
...         t.rt(90)
```

The functions fd and rt are abbreviations for forward and right. The underscore _ is used to indicate that we are not using the counter from the **for** loop. We can make a primitive star by using square multiple times:

```Python
>>> for _ in range(10):
...     square(100)
...     t.rt(360/10)
```

Here is the result:

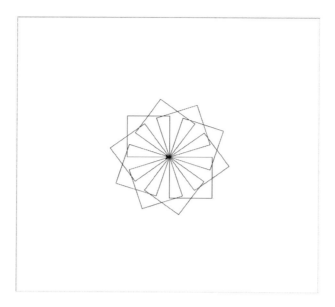

When experimenting, the methods home and clear are useful:

```Python
>>> t.home()
>>> t.clear()
```

The home method moves the turtle to the origin and restores its direction to the default. The clear function clears the turtle screen.

QUESTION 1 Write a function many_squares which, given a number of squares to use and a size for the 'star', draws it.

To make another kind of star, we can use the backward/bk method:

```
def star(l, n):
    for _ in range(n):
        t.fd(l)
        t.bk(l)
        t.rt(360/n)
```

Here is star(100, 20):

There is a left/lt equivalent to right/rt as well.

QUESTION 2 Write a function to draw a polygon with a given number of sides of a given length. Use this function, together with right turns, to repeat the given polygon multiple times to make a symmetrical pattern.

QUESTION 3 Write a function circle, which draws a circle for a given centre position and radius, choosing the number of sides dependent on size to give a smooth result. If you need π, it can be found as math.pi after using **import** math.

So far we have no way to prevent the turtle leaving a trail behind. What if we want to draw multiple stars? We can use the methods penup (stop drawing a trail) and pendown (resume drawing a trail):

```
def star(x, y, l, n):
    t.penup()
    t.home()
    t.fd(x)
    t.lt(90)
    t.fd(y)
    t.pendown()
    for _ in range(n):
        t.fd(l)
        t.bk(l)
        t.rt(360/n)
```

Now we can use the random module to draw lots of stars:

```
Python
>>>import random
>>>for _ in range(20):
...     star(random.randint(-300, 300),
...          random.randint(-300, 300),
...          random.randint(10, 150),
...          random.randint(3, 30))
```

Here is the result of one run:

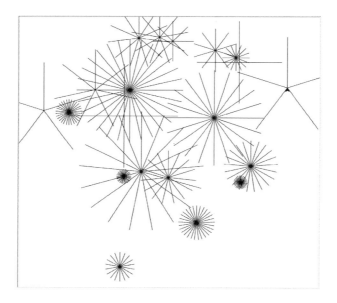

We can simplify by using the method `goto` which moves to a given coordinate directly. We also use `setheading` to start each star at a random angle:

```python
def star(x, y, l, n):
    t.penup()
    t.goto(x, y)
    t.setheading(random.randint(0,359))
    t.pendown()
    for _ in range(n):
        t.fd(l)
        t.bk(l)
        t.rt(360/n)
```

QUESTION 4 Using the goto method, write a function to draw a square grid of circles of diameter fifty which touch one another.

There are two problems with our pictures: they take a long time to draw, and the turtle gets in the way of the final result. To improve the speed, we use the speed method, which takes a number from 1 (slowest) to 10 (fastest). In addition, the number 0 means that no animation takes place, and the picture is drawn as quickly as possible. We can stop the turtle getting in the way of our final picture by using the hideturtle method (it has an opposite in showturtle). Try this:

```
Python
>>> t.hideturtle()
>>> t.speed(0)
>>> star(0, 0, 200, 7)
>>> t.showturtle()
```

The method pensize can be used to change the thickness of the trail. The pencolor method may be used to change the colour. The default pen width is 1 and, as we know, the default pen colour is black, which is the same as the red-green-blue triple $(0, 0, 0)$. Consider this sequence of commands, where we use various shades of grey from black $(0, 0, 0)$ to white $(1, 1, 1)$:

```
Python
>>> t.pensize(20)
>>> star(0, 0, 200, 7)
>>> t.pensize(15)
>>> t.color(0.25, 0.25, 0.25)
>>> star(0, 0, 200, 7)
>>> t.pensize(10)
>>> t.color(0.5, 0.5, 0.5)
>>> star(0, 0, 200, 7)
>>> t.pensize(5)
>>> t.color(0.75, 0.75, 0.75)
>>> star(0, 0, 200, 7)
>>> t.pensize(2)
>>> t.color(1, 1, 1)
>>> star(0, 0, 200, 7)
>>> t.hideturtle()
```

Here is the result:

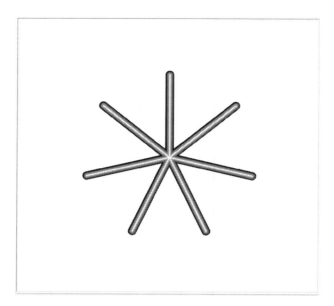

QUESTION 5 Write a program to display the whole gamut of colours available in the RGB space. That is to say, all combinations of red, green and blue, with a reasonable granularity – perhaps steps of 0.1.

The turtle module provides its own functions for drawing filled shapes:

```Python
>>> t.begin_fill()
>>> t.fd(100)
>>> t.rt(90)
>>> t.fd(100)
>>> t.rt(90)
>>> t.fd(100)
>>> t.rt(90)
>>> t.fd(100)
>>> t.end_fill()
>>> t.hideturtle()
```

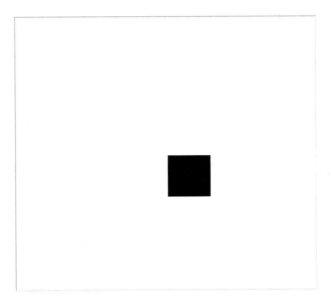

The fill colour can be set with `fillcolor`. To make a filled shape with no border, make sure the pen is up.

QUESTION 6 Modify your circle program to draw a filled circle.

Some of our arrangements of stars were prettier than others. Let us write a program to allow the user to see one after another, and when a nice one appears, to save it to file. Each image will be drawn in turn, requiring the Space key to be pressed to go to the next one. Pressing 's' instead will save the file. Pressing 'x' will quit the program. We shall be using our usual `star` function.

To begin with, we shall define three functions, to make the display, to leave the program, and to save the picture, to be triggered by the Space key, 'x' key, and 's' key respectively:

```
import sys

def many_stars():
    t.clear()
    for _ in range(20):
        star(random.randint(-300, 300),
             random.randint(-300, 300),
             random.randint(10, 150),
             random.randint(3, 30))

def stars_exit():
    sys.exit(0)

def save_stars():
    turtle.Screen().getcanvas().postscript(file='stars.ps')
    stars_exit()
```

The function `exit` from the `sys` module exits the current program (the 0 indicates an ordinary exit, as opposed to one caused by an error). It is preferable to the plain `exit()` we have been using thus far, which is intended only for use in interactive Python. The long line in `save_stars` is an incantation (which you need not understand) to save the contents of the turtle screen to the file `stars.ps`. This a so-called PostScript file, which you may open on your computer to show it. PostScript is quite an old-fashioned format, so you might need to download a program to view it.

Now, we set up the screen, hiding the turtle, setting the speed to maximum and turning animation off. We then tell the `turtle` module we wish to link certain keys to certain of our functions: they will be run each time the given key is pressed.

```
t.hideturtle()
turtle.Screen().tracer(0, 0)
turtle.Screen().onkey(save_stars, 's')
turtle.Screen().onkey(many_stars, ' ')
turtle.Screen().onkey(stars_exit, 'x')
```

Finally, we ask the turtle module to listen to the window for these keys, run our `many_stars` function once to draw the first pattern, and call `turtle.mainloop()` to begin listening for the keys.

```
turtle.listen()
many_stars()
turtle.mainloop()
```

The `turtle.mainloop()` line must be the last statement in the program. Here is the whole program:

```
import turtle
import random
import sys

def star(x, y, l, n):
    t.penup()
    t.goto(x, y)
    t.setheading(random.randint(0, 359))
    t.pendown()
    for _ in range(n):
        t.fd(l)
        t.bk(l)
        t.rt(360.0 / n)

def many_stars():
    t.clear()
    for _ in range(20):
        star(random.randint(-300, 300),
             random.randint(-300, 300),
             random.randint(10, 150),
             random.randint(3, 30))

def stars_exit():
```

```
        sys.exit(0)

def save_stars():
    turtle.Screen().getcanvas().postscript(file='stars.ps')
    stars_exit()

t = turtle.Turtle()

t.hideturtle()
turtle.Screen().tracer(0, 0)
turtle.Screen().onkey(save_stars, 's')
turtle.Screen().onkey(many_stars, ' ')
turtle.Screen().onkey(stars_exit, 'x')
turtle.listen()

manystars()
turtle.mainloop()
```

As well as key presses, we can detect mouse clicks, by using the function `Screen().onscreenclick` providing a function of which takes the *x* and *y* coordinates of the click. Here is a program to draw a star at any location clicked by the user:

```
import turtle
import random

def star(x, y, l, n):
    t.penup()
    t.goto(x, y)
    t.setheading(random.randint(0, 359))
    t.pendown()
    for _ in range(n):
        t.fd(l)
        t.bk(l)
        t.rt(360.0 / n)

def draw_star(x, y):
    star(x, y, random.randint(10, 150), random.randint(3, 30))
    turtle.Screen().update()

t = turtle.Turtle()
turtle.Screen().tracer(0, 0)
t.hideturtle()
turtle.listen()
turtle.Screen().onscreenclick(draw_star)
turtle.mainloop()
```

Now let us use what we have learned to write two more substantial programs.

PROJECT 1A: A GRAPH PLOTTER

Write a program which takes one or more formulae on the command line and plots them. For example, we might see:

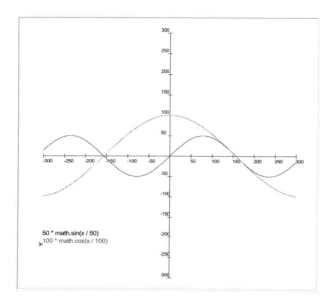

For the text on the axes, and for the labels, you will need to use the turtle function `write`. For example, the following will write the text 'Hello' at the current position in 16pt Arial:

```
Python
>>>t.write('Hello', font = ('Arial', 16, 'normal'))
```

Remember that the built-in Python function `eval` can evaluate a given piece of Python program. For example, if the variable x has value `10` the result of `eval('x * 2')` is `20`.

The answer to this first part can be found at the back of the book; answers to the following extensions are not given.

EXTENSIONS:

- Allow the axes to be set on the command line, including scaling in x and y directions.

- Use `turtle.Screen().input` to ask for the formulae, if none are given on the command line – the program is then interactive.

- Allow for the plotting of graphs using polar coordinates, graphs parameterised in terms of x and y, and so on.

PROJECT 1B: A CLOCK Write a clock program, which displays the current time on an analog clock, updating once a second. For example:

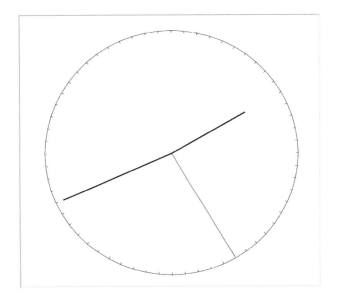

You will need the time module for this. If we have a function `clockface`, we can pass it the current time like this:

```
import time

tm = time.localtime()

clockface(tm.tm_hour, tm.tm_min, tm.tm_sec)
```

The answer to this first part can be found at the back of the book; answers to the following extensions are not given.

EXTENSIONS:

- Add the hour labels 1..12 to the clock.
- Make a prettier clock face and prettier hands, perhaps based on a clock in your house.
- Add a digital clock and an alarm function.

Project 2: Counting Calories

A popular way of failing to lose weight is to count calories. We are going to write a program to calculate and track the food and calorie intake of one or more people. For this, we will need to store information in files, and load information from others. For example, here is a very short list of foods and their calorie counts:

```
Carrots(Cooked) 100 109
Carrots(Raw) 100 111
Peas 454 350
```

The first column is the food name, the second the number of grams in question, and the third the number of calories in that number of grams. The columns are separated by spaces (and so there can be no space in the food name). This is the most common source data for calories, easy to type in, and easy to collate data from multiple sources. You can see that the Peas figure is for 454g, which is approximately one pound. A file containing the foods eaten in a single day will look like this:

```
Carrots 160
Peas 110
```

The first column is the food, the second the number of grams. The calories can be calculated by reference to the calories data file. We will also store a file containing the history of weights:

```
01-01-2020 84.3
03-01-2020 84.1
```

Here 84.3kg for 1st January and 84.1kg for 3rd January. Each person's files will be in its own directory so we might have a structure like this:

```
  │   calories.txt
  ├── robert
  │   ├── weight.txt
  │   ├── 01-01-2020.txt
  │   └── 03-01-2020.txt
  └── mary
      ├── weight.txt
      ├── 01-01-2020.txt
      ├── 02-01-2020.txt
      └── 03-01-2020.txt
```

You can build this structure yourself by typing in the data shown above (and making some up), or by downloading it from the book's website. Here is a function to read a table from a file:

```python
def table_of_file(filename):
    with open(filename) as f:
        table = {}
        for l in f.readlines():
            fields = l.split()
            key = fields[0]
            values = fields[1:]
            table[key] = values
        return table
```

You can see that we read it as a dictionary. The first column of the file makes the keys, and the values are lists of the rest of the zero or more items in each row. Everything is treated as a string, whether it represents a number or not. We have assumed the file is well-formed, and have not checked for errors. One of the exercises will be to remedy this. Here is the table of `calories.txt`:

```
{'Carrots(Cooked)': ['100', '109'],
 'Carrots(Raw)': ['100', '111'],
 'Peas': ['100', '350']}
```

We can write a function to print the foods out in a nicer format:

```python
def list_foods():
    for k, vs in table_of_file('calories.txt').items():
        print(k, end=' ')
        for v in vs: print(v, end=' ')
        print('')
```

Here is the result:

```
Python
>>> list_foods()
Carrots(Cooked) 100 109
Carrots(Raw) 100 111
Peas 100 350
```

The function `os.path.join` which we can access by using **import** `os` can be used to construct the full path to a file given its directory and file name. For example, `os.path.join('robert', 'weight.txt')` might produce `'robert/weight.txt'` (the exact result will depend on your system). We can use this to list the foods eaten on a particular day:

```
import os

def list_eaten(name, date):
    for k, vs in table_of_file(os.path.join(name, date) + '.txt').items():
        print(f'{k} {vs[0]}')
```

QUESTION 1 Write a function `list_weights` to list the contents of the `weight.txt` file, given the name of the user.

QUESTION 2 Write a function `list_dates` to list the dates for which we have calorie data for a given user. The function `os.listdir('robert')`, for example, will produce an (unsorted) list of the files in the directory `robert`.

Now we can write a function to look up the number of calories for a given food in `calories.txt`:

```
def lookup_calories(food):
    table = table_of_file('calories.txt')
    vs = table[food]
    if vs is None:
        print(f'Food {food} not found')
    else:
        if len(vs) > 1:
            weight = vs[0]
            calories = vs[1]
            print(f'There are {calories} calories in {weight}g of {food}')
        else:
            print(f'Malformed calorie entry for {food} in calories file')
```

We have used dictionary lookup to locate the weight and calories for the food, and then slicing to extract them from the list.

QUESTION 3 Write a function `lookup_weight` which, given a name and a date, prints the weight at that date, if available.

To calculate the total calories for a given date, we must combine data from the user's food records for that date with the calorie data:

```
def total_date(name, date):
    calories = table_of_file('calories.txt')
    table = table_of_file(os.path.join(name, date) + '.txt')
    total = 0
    for k, vs in table.items():
        weight_and_calories = calories[k]
        reference_weight = int(weight_and_calories[0])
        reference_calories = int(weight_and_calories[1])
        calories_per_gram = reference_calories / reference_weight
        total += int(vs[0]) * calories_per_gram
```

QUESTION 4 Write a function new_user which, given a name, makes a new directory for that person, and creates an empty weight.txt file. You will need the function os.mkdir which, given a name, makes a directory.

So far, we have been able to treat dates like any other kind of string, without regard to their meaning. However, to add data to the correct file, we would like the user to be able to avoid typing the date – the data should be added to the file with today's date. We use a function from the datetime module:

```
import datetime

def date_today():
    d = datetime.datetime.now()
    return f'{d.day:02}-{d.month:02}-{d.year}'
```

The structure d contains today's time and date. We extract the day, month, and year, making sure to format the day and month to two character each (i.e. to include leading zeroes). Now we can use our new date_today function to write a functions to add data for today, using the append file mode:

```
def eaten(name, food, grams):
    with open(os.path.join(name, date_today()) + '.txt', 'a') as f:
        print(f'{food} {grams}', file=f)

def weighed(name, weight):
    with open(os.path.join(name, 'weight.txt'), 'a') as f:
        print(f'{date_today()} {weight}', file=f)
```

The program will be run from the command line by writing python cals.py followed by the command and any extra data required. Here are the commands:

Command	Description
`list eaten <name> <date>`	List foods eaten on a given date.
`list weights <name>`	List the weight history for a user.
`list dates <name>`	List the dates for which there are calorie counts.
`list foods`	List all calorie data for known foods.
`lookup calories <food>`	Look up calories for a given food.
`lookup weight <name> <date>`	Look up weight for given date.
`total <name> <date>`	Calculate total calories for a given user and date.
`newuser <name>`	Create a new user.
`eaten <name> <food> <weight>`	Add food data for today.
`weighed <name> <weight>`	Add weight data for today.

A rather convoluted construction implements this, dispatching to the functions we have already written (see overleaf). There are, as you might expect, Python libraries to deal with this sort of task and, if our program became any more complicated, we would switch to one of them.

QUESTION 5 In many of our functions, we have not checked for errors. For example, do files exist? Are they in the correct format? Is the command line correct? Try to enumerate all the possible errors requiring detection. Pick one or two functions and fix them to deal with such errors.

A standard data format

We have been using our own ad-hoc representation for our data files; but there is an longstanding industry standard: the CSV or Comma-Separated Values format. This is rather like our own format, but adds a line at the top with column titles, and allows entries to have spaces inside them, if they are surrounded by quotation marks:

```
Food,Weight,Calories
"Carrots, Cooked",100,109
"Carrots, Raw",100,111
"Peas",100,350
```

The advantage of using this standard format, is that we can replace our own table handling functions with the Python CSV library. In addition, we can use the CSV files created by our program to export data to other programs, for example a spreadsheet. Here is our calories CSV file, imported into Microsoft Excel, for example:

A1		f_x	Food	
	A	B	C	
1	Food	Weight	Calories	
2	Carrots, Cooked	100	109	
3	Carrots, Raw	100	111	
4	Peas	100	350	
5				

```
import sys

if len(arg) > 1:
    cmd = arg[1]
    if cmd == 'list':
        if len(arg) > 3 and arg[2] == 'eaten':
            list_eaten(arg[3], arg[4])
        else:
            if arg[2] == 'weights' and len(arg) > 3:
                list_weights(arg[3])
            elif arg[2] == 'dates' and len(arg) > 3:
                list_dates(arg[3])
            elif arg[2] == 'foods':
                list_foods()
    elif cmd == 'lookup':
        if len(arg) > 2:
            if arg[2] == 'calories':
                lookup_calories(arg[3])
            elif arg[2] == 'weight' and len(arg) > 3:
                lookup_weight(arg[3], arg[4])
    elif cmd == 'total':
        if len(arg) > 3:
            total_date(arg[2], arg[3])
    elif cmd == 'newuser':
        if len(arg) > 2:
            new_user(arg[2])
    elif cmd == 'eaten':
        if len(arg) > 4:
            eaten(arg[2], arg[3], arg[4])
    elif cmd == 'weighed':
        if len(arg) > 3:
            weighed(arg[2], arg[3])
    else:
        print('Command not understood')
```

How do we convert our `cals.py` program into the new `csvcals.py` program? First we import the csv module and modify our `table_of_file` function:

```
import csv

def table_of_file(filename):
    with open(filename) as c:
        r = csv.reader(c)                    read the CSV data
        next(r)                              skip the row of column names
        table = {}
        for row in r:
            table[row[0]] = row[1:]          load a row's key and values
        return table
```

Now it is very easy to modify our other functions to change the filenames to `.csv`. Because we have modified `table_of_file` function, all our table-reading and processing functions work just fine:

```
def list_eaten(name, date):
    for k, vs in table_of_file(os.path.join(name, date) + '.csv').items():
        print(f'{k} {vs[0]}')
```

The places where we do need to make more significant changes are in the functions which create new files. We must add the column headings:

```
def new_user(name):
    os.mkdir(name)
    with open(os.path.join(name, 'weight.csv'), 'w') as f:
        print('Date,Weight', file=f)
```

We must put quotation marks around the food name, and add the CSV header if the file does not already exist, using the function `os.path.exists`, which checks if a file or directory already exists:

```
def eaten(name, food, grams):
    filename = os.path.join(name, date_today()) + '.csv'
    is_new = not os.path.exists(filename)
    with open(filename, 'a') as f:
        if is_new: print('Food,Weight', file=f)
        print(f'"{food}",{grams}', file=f)

def weighed(name, weight):
    filename = os.path.join(name, 'weight.csv')
    is_new = not os.path.exists(filename)
    with open(filename, 'a') as f:
        if is_new: print('Date,Weight', file=f)
        print(f'{date_today()},{weight}', file=f)
```

This completes the modifications.

QUESTION 6 Complete the conversion of our `cals.py` program into `csvcals.py`, and test it.

QUESTION 7 Locate the Python CSV module documentation online, and use it to alter our `csvcals.py` program to write files using functions provided by that module, as well as read using them.

Project 3: Noughts and Crosses

The childhood game of Noughts and Crosses is a combinatorial problem of a large but manageable size. Let us review the rules, and then see if we can build the *game tree* (that is, a structure describing all possible games), and draw some statistics from it.

A 3-by-3 grid is constructed. Two players (O and X) take turns to place their piece in an empty space. The game is won if or when a player forms three pieces in a row, column, or diagonally. The game is drawn if the board is full and no such pattern has been formed. For example, in this board, player O has won, building a diagonal:

	X	O
	O	X
O	X	O

QUESTION 1 Games of size 1-by-1 and 2-by-2 are uninteresting. Why?

QUESTION 2 From your own experience, can you write down some rules to help a beginning player win (or avoid losing) a 3-by-3 game of Noughts and Crosses?

Representing the board

We can assign a number to each position in the board:

0	1	2
3	4	5
6	7	8

The board can be represented as a simple list of strings, one for each position 0..8 in the board. In the empty board, all positions have the string '_'.

```
emptyboard = ['_', '_', '_', '_', '_', '_', '_', '_', '_']
```

You might wonder why we do not use a list of lists of length three to represent rows. This does not in fact simplify the problem, since we need to talk about columns and diagonals just as often. We can print the board out:

```
def print_board(b):
    for n, x in enumerate(b):
        print(x, end='')
        if n % 3 == 0: print('')
```

We will need some simple functions to determine properties of a board. To test when a board is full (i.e. when the game is drawn) is easy:

```
def full(b):
    return '_' not in b
```

Calculating whether a particular player has won is rather harder, since we need to check each horizontal line, vertical line, and diagonal. We can enumerate these lines:

```
h1 = [0, 1, 2]                                             horizontal
h2 = [3, 4, 5]
h3 = [6, 7, 8]
v1 = [0, 3, 6]                                             vertical
v2 = [1, 4, 7]
v3 = [2, 5, 8]
d1 = [0, 4, 8]                                             diagonal
d2 = [2, 4, 6]

lines = [h1, h2, h3, v1, v2, v3, d1, d2]
```

Now we can look up each line's positions in the board, and compare it with what a winning line would look like:

```
def wins(p, b):
    win = [p, p, p]                                       a winning line
    for l in lines:
        bl = [b[x] for x in l]                            extract the line
        if bl == win: return True
    return False                                          no line matched
```

QUESTION 3 Write a function random_move which plays a given piece in a blank space, chosen at random. Now write a function random_game which uses it to play an arbitrary, but valid, game. The game should end when it is won or drawn, even if the board is not yet full. Print the game as it progresses.

Human players

The human player plays '0'. The human_move function asks the user to select a board position for the next '0', making sure to check the user's input is sensible. Then it fills in the space on the board.

```
Python
>>> b = ['_', 'X', '_', '_', '_', '_', '_', '_', '_']
>>> human_move(b)
Position 0..8? six
Not a valid board position
Position 0..8? 9
Board position must be from 0..8
Position 0..8? 5
>>> b
['_', 'X', '_', '_', '_', '0', '_', '_', '_']
```

QUESTION 4 Write the function human_move matching this description. The built-in method isdigit on strings may be used to check if a string represents a digit.

QUESTION 5 Extend the function to play either 'X' or '0'. Now write a program allowing two humans to play one another. Print the empty board at the beginning, and the board after each turn. Print which player won, or if it was a draw.

Computer players

In question 3, we wrote a very simple random computer player. This is a player against which a human would almost always win. As we know from experience, however, even a child can learn easily how to win (or force a draw) in any game of 3x3 Noughts and Crosses, whether they place the first piece or not.

We can imagine a computer strategy as a list of types of move to make, in order of importance. For example, the most important rule might be that, if we can win, we make the winning play. The next, failing that, might be to play in a position which blocks the other player winning at the next turn. If that is not possible, we might choose to take the centre square, if it is free. And so on, until we find a move we can make.

We will build a series of 'tactics'. Each tactic will assess whether it can be applied. If not, it will return False. Otherwise it will place the piece, and return True.

Let us implement the tactic of choosing the centre space for computer player 'X' if it is available, for example. First, we write a function to take the first space, if any is available, from a list to try:

```
def try_to_take(b, ps):
    for p in ps:
        if b[p] == '_':
            b[p] = 'X'
            return True
    return False
```

Then, the tactic itself is simple:

```python
def tactic_play_centre(b):
    return try_to_take(b, [4])
```

The 'win' and 'block' tactics are in fact similar to one another – if there is one space in a line, and two of our pieces we can win. If there is one space, and two of our opponents pieces, we must block. So we can write a single function which checks for this situation:

```python
def win_or_block(b, piece):
    for l in lines:
        bl = [b[x] for x in l]
        if bl.count('_') == 1 and bl.count(piece) == 2:
            for x in l:
                if b[x] == '_': b[x] = 'X'
            return True
    return False
```

Then the win and block tactics are simple:

```python
def tactic_win(b):
    return win_or_block(b, 'X')

def tactic_block(b):
    return win_or_block(b, 'O')
```

We need a last-resort tactic which simply plays the first blank space:

```python
def tactic_first_blank(b):
    return try_to_take(b, [0, 1, 2, 3, 4, 5, 6, 7, 8])
```

Now we can string the tactics together to build our `computer_move` function:

```python
def computer_move(b):
    print('Computer has played:')
    if tactic_win(b):
        print('Used tactic_win')
        return
    if tactic_block(b):
        print('Used tactic_block')
        return
    if tactic_play_centre(b):
        print('Used tactic_centre')
        return
    if tactic_first_blank(b):
        print('Used tactic_first_blank')
        return
    print('No tactic applied: error in tactic implementations')
```

Note that the **return** construct is used here to end the function early, not to return a value.

There is in fact a full, foolproof strategy for winning or forcing a draw. It consists, as we have suggested, of a list of rules to apply in turn, taking the first one which works. Here is the description, from "Flexible Strategy Use in Young Children's Tic-Tac-Toe" by Kevin Crowley and Robert S. Siegler:

Model of Expert Performance

Win
> *If* there is a row, column, or diagonal with two of my pieces and a blank space,
> *Then* play the blank space (thus winning the game).

Block
> *If* there is a row, column, or diagonal with two of my opponent's pieces and a blank space,
> *Then* play the blank space (thus blocking a potential win for my opponent).

Fork
> *If* there are two intersecting rows, columns, or diagonals with one of my pieces and two blanks, and
> *If* the intersecting space is empty,
> *Then* move to the intersecting space (thus creating two ways to win on my next turn).

Block Fork
> *If* there are two intersecting rows, columns, or diagonals with one of my opponent's pieces and two blanks, and
> *If* the intersecting space is empty,
> *Then*
>> *If* there is an empty location that creates a two-in-a-row for me (thus forcing my opponent to block rather than fork),
>> *Then* move to the location.
>> *Else* move to the intersection space (thus occupying the location that my opponent could use to fork).

Play Center
> *If* the center is blank,
> *Then* play the center.

Play Opposite Corner
> *If* my opponent is in a corner, and
> *If* the opposite corner is empty,
> *Then* play the opposite corner.

Play Empty Corner
> *If* there is an empty corner,
> *Then* move to an empty corner.

Play Empty Side
> *If* there is an empty side,
> *Then* move to an empty side.

You can see that the 'Win', 'Block' and 'Center' rules are the ones we have already implemented.

QUESTION 6 Add the Empty Corner and Empty Side rules, allowing us to remove our First Blank rule. Add the Opposite Corner rule.

QUESTION 7 Make a human-vs-computer game using your new player. Allow either player to make the first move, and make sure to print the intermediate and final state of the board.

QUESTION 8 Implement the remaining two tactics, Fork and Block Fork, which are rather more complicated.

All possible games

How many possible different games of Noughts and Crosses are there? How often does the player going first win, how often the playing going second, and how often is the game drawn? To answer these questions and more, we will construct what is known as a game tree. It is called a tree because it has a branching structure.

Let us consider the shape of the game tree when X begins. Clearly, at the top level, it will branch nine ways, since the starting player X can be placed in any square. Then eight ways, seven ways and so on. Once we reach the fifth level, some of the games have been won (since three pieces from player X may form a line), and so the number of branches may be reduced. The tree must end after nine levels, since the board must at least be full, even if no-one has won. Here is a fragment of the game tree:

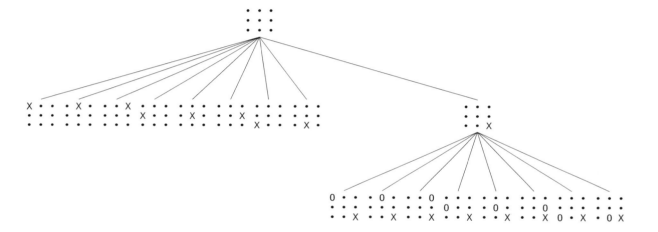

How can we represent and construct the tree? We shall need to swap between players at each level to simulate turns, so we write a simple function for that:

```
def swap_player(p):
    if p == 'X': return 'O'
    else: return 'X'
```

Our data structure for the tree will be a pair (b, bs) where b is the current board, and bs a list of trees representing the possible successor trees after a move has taken place.

The function to build this tree is therefore recursive, just like the data structure. First it checks to see if the current board is won or drawn, in which case there are no successor boards. Otherwise, we produce a sub-tree for each possible move i.e. for each possible blank space in the board. We return the pairs of the board and the list of successor trees (produced by recursion), swapping the player each time.

```
def next_boards(b, pl):
    if wins('0', b) or wins('X', b) or full(b):
        return (b, [])
    bs = []
    for i, e in enumerate(b):
        if e == '_':
            new_board = b.copy()
            new_board[i] = pl
            bs.append(new_board)
    return (b, [next_boards(x, swap_player(pl)) for x in bs])
```

We must be careful to copy the board using the list method copy, so that each list is mutated separately. Now we just need to set the process in motion, beginning with the empty board:

```
def game_tree(pl):
    return next_boards(emptyboard, pl)

x_game_tree = game_tree('X')
```

This takes quite some time to run. The result is far too large to read on screen (you can print it just by writing x_game_tree and pressing Enter). We will therefore have to write some functions to interrogate the tree to derive statistics from it. For example, the following function tells us that X wins a game started by X 131184 times.

```
def sum_x_wins(t):
    b, bs = t
    ns = wins('X', b)
    for board in bs:
        ns += sum_x_wins(board)
    return ns

x_wins = sum_x_wins(x_game_tree)
```

Here, we are making use of the fact that True can be considered by Python to be the integer 1, and False the integer 0 when performing addition.

QUESTION 9 In how many cases does O win? How many games end in a draw? How many possible different games are there?

QUESTION 10 Write a function sum_game_tree(f, t) which takes a function and a tree, and gives the number of items in the tree for which the function is true. Use this to remove duplicate parts of your functions from question 9.

QUESTION 11 Another use for a tree is in connection with our Morse code example from chapter 3. We can build a tree of our codes like this:

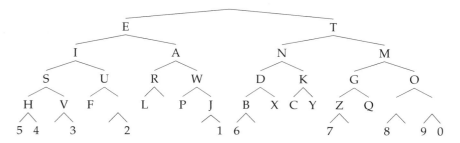

Each line to the left is a dot, each to the right a dash. Encode this tree in Python, and use it to write a decoder for our Morse messages.

Project 4: Photo Finish

Earlier, we drew pictures by having a turtle draw lines. In this chapter, we consider another kind of image: photographic ones, which are made up of millions of little 'pixels' (picture elements) in a square grid. Here is such a picture (in colour in the electronic version of this book, in black and white in the printed version):

This picture has 200 rows and 200 columns, making in total 40,000 pixels, each of which is an (r, g, b) triple where red, green, and blue range from 0 (no light of that colour) to 255 (full light of that colour) inclusive. You can download this picture from the book's website, or find one of your own. It must have a file name ending .png and should not have any transparent elements (we will see how to check this soon).

This chapter, unlike every other chapter in this book, requires installing some external software, namely the Pillow library for Python. Installation instructions depend upon your computer, and may change over time, so the author can only direct you to the internet. You will know you have it installed properly when the following does not give an error:

```Python
>>> from PIL import Image
```

This is a version of the **import** construct we have not yet seen. It provides access to just the Image sub-module of the Pillow library. Now we can open the image:

```Python
>>> i = Image.open('rabbit.png')
```

The Pillow module has a built in method to show an image on screen. How it is shown depends on your system – typically it is opened in whichever program is set as the default program to show PNG files.

```
Python
>>> i.show()
```

The method `load` on the image gives us access to the actual pixels, and `size` gives us the number of
rows and columns. We get the value of a pixel at a given coordinate by writing `p[x, y]` where `p` is the
result of `load`. Let us make the image greyscale by averaging the red, green, and blue values for each
pixel:

```
p = i.load()
sx, sy = i.size
for x in range(sx):
    for y in range(sy):
        r, g, b = p[x, y]
        gr = int((r + g + b) / 3)
        p[x, y] = (gr, gr, gr)          we also set pixels using p[x, y]
```

If you accidentally chose a PNG file with transparency, you will see an error similar to this:

```
Python
Traceback (most recent call last):
  File "<stdin>", line 3, in <module>
ValueError: too many values to unpack (expected 3)
```

We can save it to a new file:

```
Python
>>> i.save('greyrabbit.png')
```

We might like to write several functions of this type, so it makes sense to split up the idea of processing
all the pixels in-place from the calculation done on each pixel. Let us write a `grey` function:

```
def grey(p):
    r, g, b = p
    gr = int((r + g + b) / 3)
    return (gr, gr, gr)
```

Now we can write `process_pixels_in_place` which takes a function such as `grey` and an image,
and processes each pixel using the function:

```
def process_pixels_in_place(f, i):
    p = i.load()
    sx, sy = i.size
    for x in range(sx):
        for y in range(sy):
            p[x, y] = f(p[x, y])
```

Now we can use it like this:

Python
```
>>> process_pixels_in_place(grey, i)
```

QUESTION 1 Write functions to increase or decrease the brightness and contrast of an image. Brightness may be achieved by simple addition of each component of each pixel by an appropriate factor, and contrast by multiplication.

QUESTION 2 Write functions to flip an image vertically or horizontally, and to rotate an image by 180 degrees, all in-place.

We have loaded one image, modified it, and saved it. But how do we make a new image, or combine images? Let us write a function to add a border to an image, like a picture frame:

```python
def border(i, width, colour):
    sx, sy = i.size
    p = i.load()
    i2 = Image.new('RGB', (sx + width * 2, sy + width * 2), colour)
    p2 = i2.load()
    for x in range(sx):
        for y in range(sy):
            p2[x + width, y + width] = p[x, y]
    return i2
```

The function `border` adds a border of a given width and colour to an image, returning a new image. The original is unaltered. We use the `Image.new` method to build a new image of larger dimensions, filled with the frame colour. Then, we copy the pixels one-by-one. Now we can use it:

Python
```
>>> bordered = border(i, 20, (150, 150, 150))
```

Here is the result:

We can blur an image, to make it look out of focus, by making each pixel the average of its eight surrounding pixels and itself:

```python
def blur(i):
    p = i.load()
    i2 = i.copy()
    p2 = i2.load()
    sx, sy = i.size
    for x in range(1, sx - 1):
        for y in range(1, sy - 1):
            sumr, sumg, sumb = 0, 0, 0
            for dx in range(-1, 2):
                for dy in range(-1, 2):
                    sourcer, sourceg, sourceb = p[x + dx, y + dy]
                    sumr += sourcer
                    sumg += sourceg
                    sumb += sourceb
            p2[x, y] = (int(sumr / 9), int(sumg / 9), int(sumb / 9))
    return i2
```

Here we have used the copy method to make, and thus return, a new image of the same size. Now we can use it a few times, making sure to begin with an image bordered in white, so that there is room for the blurring:

```
Python
>>> white_bordered = border(i, 20, (255, 255, 255))
>>> x = blur(blur(blur(white_bordered)))
>>> x.save('blurred.png')
```

Here is the result:

QUESTION 3 Rewrite the blurring to work in-place. Is the result appreciably different?

QUESTION 4 How wide does the border have to be for any given number of blurring operations? Implement a version which uses only the border required.

We have only looked at still pictures so far: Pillow has some facilities for dealing with basic moving pictures in the form of the animated GIFs we are all so familiar with from the internet. We are going to fade our image out to white over the course of a number of 'frames' making up a short animated GIF.

Since we will need to keep multiple images, each processed differently, we shall need a version of our pixel-processor which does not work in-place, but rather returns a new, processed image:

```
def process_pixels(f, i):
    p = i.load()
    i2 = i.copy()
    p2 = i2.load()
    sx, sy = i.size
    for x in range(sx):
        for y in range(sy):
            p2[x, y] = f(p[x, y])
    return i2
```

Here is the function to fade towards white by a given factor from 0 to 100. With a pen and paper, or your computer, can you verify it is correct?

```
def fade_by(f, p):
    r, g, b = p
    r_out = int((f * r + (100 - f) * 255) / 100)
    g_out = int((f * g + (100 - f) * 255) / 100)
    b_out = int((f * b + (100 - f) * 255) / 100)
    return (r_out, g_out, b_out)
```

Now we can collect images for each level of fade from 100 down to 0 in steps of 5:

```
def make_images(i):
    images = []
    for x in range(100, -1, -5):
        def fade(p): return fade_by(x, p)
        faded = process_pixels(fade, i)
        images.append(faded)
    return images
```

We use the function to build the faded images from our original, and save the animated GIF:

```
Python
>>> images = make_images(i)
>>> images[0].save('fade.gif', save_all=True, append_images=images[1:],
                    duration=100, loop=0)
```

The mechanism to save the GIF is not intuitive: it is a method on the first image, listing the rest of the images. The duration is the number of milliseconds between frames, that is to say one tenth of a second. Here are frames 1, 10, and 15:

QUESTION 5 Produce a GIF of your picture, being blurred repeatedly, perhaps 100 times. You will notice that the result is a little grainy – GIFs can have only 256 colours in them, for historical reasons.

Answers to Questions

Hints may be found on page 221.

Chapter 1 (Starting Off)

1

The expression 17 is a number and so is a value already – there is no work to do. The expression 1 + 2 * 3 + 4 will evaluate to the value 11, since multiplication has higher precedence than addition. The expression 400 > 200 evaluates to the boolean True since this is result of the comparison operator > on the operands 400 and 200. Similarly, 1 != 1 evaluates to False. The expression True **or** False evaluates to True since one of the operands is true. Similarly, True **and** False evaluates to False since one of the operands is false. The expression '%' is a string and is already a value.

2

The expression evaluates to 11. The programmer seems to be under the impression that spacing affects precedence. It does not, and so this use of space is misleading.

3

The % operator is of higher precedence than the + operator. So 1 + 2 % 3 and 1 + (2 % 3) are the same expression, evaluating to 1 + 2 which is 3, but (1 + 2) % 3 is the same as 3 % 3, which is 0.

4

The comparison operator < considers the words in dictionary order, so 'bacon' < 'eggs'. The uppercase letters are all "smaller" than the lowercase characters, so for example 'Bacon' < 'Bacon' evaluates to True. For booleans, False is considered "less than" True.

5

The first one is, of course entirely as expected:

```
Python
>>> 1 + 2
3
```

It turns out that the + operator we have been using on numbers to add them can be used on strings to concatenate them:

```
Python
>>> 'one' + 'two'
'onetwo'
```

However, it will not work to mix the two types:

```
Python
>>> 1 + 'two'
Traceback (most recent call last):
  File "<stdin>", line 1, in <module>
TypeError: unsupported operand type(s) for +: 'int' and 'str'
```

The * operator can also be used on a string and a number, to concatenate the string multiple times:

```
Python
>>> 3 * '1'
'111'
>>> '1' * 3
'111'
>>> print('1' * 3)
111
```

In the last line, we remember the difference between a string and printing a string. When it is (ab)used as a number, True has the value 1, whereas False has the value 0:

```
Python
>>> True + 1
2
>>> False + 1
1
```

Did you notice the f before the quotation mark in the last example? This is a *format string*, which we will discuss in chapter 6:

```
Python
>>> print(f'One and two is {1 + 2} and that is all.')
One and two is 3 and that is all.
```

The part between the curly braces {} has been evaluated and then printed.

Chapter 2 (Names and Functions)

1

We include the **return** keyword to make sure the result is returned to us:

```
Python
>>> def times_ten(x):
...     return x * 10
...
>>> times_ten(50)
500
```

2

This function will have two arguments. We use the **and** operator, together with the inequality operator !=.

```
Python
>>> def both_non_zero(a, b):
...     return a != 0 and b != 0
...
>>> both_non_zero(1, 2)
True
>>> both_non_zero(1, 0)
False
```

3

This is a simple function with three arguments. We remember to use **return**, of course:

```
Python
>>> def volume(w, h, d):
...     return w * h * d
...
>>> volume(10, 20, 30)
6000
```

We can now write our volume_ten_deep function:

```
Python
>>> def volume_ten_deep(w, h):
...     return volume(w, h, 10)
>>> volume_ten_deep(5, 6)
300
```

Notice that we need **return** here too: the **return** in volume will not suffice.

4

If a lower case character in the range 'a'...'z' is not a vowel, it must be a consonant. So we can reuse the is_vowel function we wrote earlier, and negate its result using **not**:

```Python
>>> def is_consonant(s):
...     return not is_vowel(s)
...
>>> is_consonant('r')
True
>>> is_consonant('e')
False
```

5

We could simply return 0 for a negative argument. The factorial of 0 is 1, so we can change that too, and say our new function finds the factorial of any non-negative number:

```Python
>>> def factorial(x):
...     if x < 0:
...         return 0
...     elif x == 0:
...         return 1
...     else:
...         return x * factorial(x - 1)
...
>>> factorial(-1)
0
```

6

We can use a recursive function:

```Python
>>> def sum_nums(n):
...     if n == 1:
...         return 1
...     else:
...         return n + sum_nums(n - 1)
...
>>> sum_nums(10)
55
```

There is a direct mathematical formula too. We use the integer division operator //, which we have not yet seen:

```
Python
>>> def sum_nums(n):
...     return (n * (n + 1)) // 2
>>> sum_nums(10)
55
```

Can you see why?

7

A number to the power of 0 is 1. A number to the power of 1 is itself. Otherwise, the answer is the current n multiplied by n^{x-1}.

```
Python
>>> def power(x, n):
...     if n == 0:
...         return 1
...     else:
...         if n == 1:
...             return x
...         else:
...             return x * power(x, n - 1)
...
>>> power(2, 5)
32
```

Notice that we had to put one **if** and **else** inside another here. The indentation helps to show the structure. Remembering that Python allows us to compress this using the **elif** keyword:

```
Python
>>> def power(x, n):
...     if n == 0:
...         return 1
...     elif n == 1:
...         return x
...     else:
...         return x * power(x, n - 1)
...
>>> power(2, 5)
32
```

This is easier to read, partly because all the **return** keywords line up. In fact, we can remove the case for n = 1 since power(x, 1) will reduce to x * power(x, 0) which is just x.

8

We test each number less than the given number for divisibility using the % modulus operator we learned about in chapter 1, increasing the test divisor by one each time. If it is divisible, we print it.

```Python
>>> def factors(n, x):
...   if x % n == 0: print(n)
...   if n < x: factors(n + 1, x)
>>> factors(1, 12)
1
2
3
4
6
12
```

We can clean the solution up by wrapping it in another function which supplies the starting point of 1:

```Python
>>> def factors_simple(x):
...     factors(1, x)
>>> factors_simple(12)
1
2
3
4
6
12
```

Chapter 3 (Again and Again)

1

We set the step to −1. We must be careful with the start and stop points. We set the stop point to 0 so that we stop at 1 (i.e. before we get to 0):

```
def print_down_from(n):
    for x in range(n, 0, -1):
        print(x)
```

2

We change the calculation of column_width to take n * (n - 1) as the item with maximum width rather than n * n:

```
def times_table(n):
    column_width = len(str(n * (n - 1))) + 1
    for y in range(1, n + 1):
        for x in range(1, n + 1):
            print(x * y, end=' ' * (column_width - len(str(x * y))))
        print('')
```

Here is the new result for a table of size ten:

Python
```
>>> times_table(10)
1  2  3  4  5  6  7  8  9  10
2  4  6  8  10 12 14 16 18 20
3  6  9  12 15 18 21 24 27 30
4  8  12 16 20 24 28 32 36 40
5  10 15 20 25 30 35 40 45 50
6  12 18 24 30 36 42 48 54 60
7  14 21 28 35 42 49 56 63 70
8  16 24 32 40 48 56 64 72 80
9  18 27 36 45 54 63 72 81 90
10 20 30 40 50 60 70 80 90 100
```

It is still possible to have excess space in some columns with this method:

Python
```
>>> times_table(4)
1  2  3  4
2  4  6  8
3  6  9  12
4  8  12 16
```

Can you fix this?

3

We use a **for** loop to check each letter in the string, adding one to a local variable each time we see a space:

```
def count_spaces(s):
    c = 0
    for x in s:
        if x == ' ':
            c = c + 1
    return c
```

We use **return** to make sure the final count is the result of the function. We can use the += operator to shorten the common operation of adding to a variable:

```
def count_spaces(s):
    c = 0
    for x in s:
        if x == ' ':
            c += 1
    return c
```

This works for other operators too.

4

This is a classic problem. It sounds easy, and yet requires several changes. We calculate the length of the string with len, so we know how many letters there are left to go. Then, in the **for** loop itself, we deduct one from that count each time, and print the space only if the count indicates we are not on the last letter.

```
def print_spaced(s):
    l = len(s)
    for x in s:
        print(x, end='')
        l = l - 1
        if l > 0:
            print(' ', end='')
```

5

A very simple **while** loop is required:

```
def sentence_checker():
    text = 'Jackdaws love my sphinx of Quartz'
    print(text)
    while input() != text:
        print('Incorrect! Try again...')
    print('Correct!')
```

6

We supply the prompt directly to the input function. We must add the newline \n because, unlike print, input does not move to the next line after printing the prompt.

```
def ask_for_password():
    entered = ''
    while entered != 'please':
        entered = input('Please enter the password\n')
```

We can now remove the entered variable, but we must use **pass**, otherwise the **while** statement would be ungrammatical in Python:

```
def ask_for_password():
    while input('Please enter the password\n') != 'please':
        pass
```

7

We need three variables: target to hold the secret number between 1 and 100, guess to hold the current guess, and tries to count the number of tries.

```
import random

def guessing_game():
    target = random.randint(1, 100)
    guess = int(input('Guess a number between 1 and 100\n'))
    tries = 1
    while guess != target:
        tries = tries + 1
        if guess < target:
            guess = int(input('Higher!\n'))
        elif guess > target:
            guess = int(input('Lower!\n'))
    print('Correct! You took ' + str(tries) + ' guesses.')
```

Inside the **while** loop, we add one to the number of tries, and keep going until the correct answer is guessed. Then we print the final message with the number of tries. Notice that we have use an **if** and an **elif** but no **else**. Can you simplify the conditional construct further?

8

We use one giant **if** construct (in the next chapter we shall discuss better ways to do this). The function print_morse_letter prints a single code for the given letter, followed by three spaces:

```
def print_morse_letter(l):
    if l == 'A': print('. -', end='    ')
    elif l == 'B': print('- . . .', end='    ')
    elif l == 'C': print('- . - .', end='    ')
    elif l == 'D': print('- . .', end='   ')
    elif l == 'E': print('.', end='    ')
    elif l == 'F': print('. . - .', end='    ')
    elif l == 'G': print('- - .', end='   ')
    elif l == 'H': print('. . . .', end='    ')
    elif l == 'I': print('. .', end='    ')
    elif l == 'J': print('. - - -', end='    ')
    elif l == 'K': print('- . -', end='    ')
    elif l == 'L': print('. - . .', end='    ')
    elif l == 'M': print('- -', end='    ')
    elif l == 'N': print('- .', end='    ')
    elif l == 'O': print('- - -', end='    ')
    elif l == 'P': print('. - - .', end='    ')
    elif l == 'Q': print('- -. -', end='   ')
    elif l == 'R': print('- . -', end='    ')
    elif l == 'S': print('. . .', end='    ')
    elif l == 'T': print('-', end='    ')
    elif l == 'U': print('. . -', end='    ')
    elif l == 'V': print('. . . -', end='    ')
    elif l == 'W': print('. - -', end='    ')
    elif l == 'X': print('- . . -', end='    ')
    elif l == 'Y': print('- . - -', end='    ')
    elif l == 'Z': print('- - . .', end='    ')
    elif l == '1': print('. - - - -', end='    ')
    elif l == '2': print('. . - - -', end='    ')
    elif l == '3': print('. . . - -', end='    ')
    elif l == '4': print('. . . . -', end='    ')
    elif l == '5': print('. . . . .', end='    ')
    elif l == '6': print('- . . . .', end='    ')
    elif l == '7': print('- - . . .', end='    ')
    elif l == '8': print('- - - . .', end='    ')
    elif l == '9': print('- - - - .', end='    ')
    elif l == '0': print('- - - - -', end='    ')
    else: print('bad letter')
```

Now the main function, to print a whole string, uses `print_morse_letter` for each letter which is not a space. For spaces it prints an extra four spaces in the output to add to the three following the previous letter.

```
def print_morse(s):
    for l in s:
        if l == ' ': print('    ', end='')
        else: print_morse_letter(l)
    print('')
```

This implementation has two problems: (1) it prints an extra three spaces at the end of any message not ending with a space; and (2) a space at the beginning of a message will have only four spaces in the output not seven. Can you fix them?

Chapter 4 (Making Lists)

1

The `first` function is simple: we just return the element at index 0. To return the last element we must use the `len` function to calculate the index. We remember to subtract one, since list indices start at zero.

```
def first(l):
    return l[0]

def last(l):
    return l[len(l) - 1]
```

In fact, we can also write `l[-1]` to retrieve the last element of a list in Python. What happens in each case if the list is empty?

2

We first create a fresh, empty list. Then we can iterate over the input list in order, inserting each element at index 0 in the new list. The effect is to produce a reversed list, which is then returned.

```
def reverse(l):
    l2 = []
    for x in l:
        l2.insert(0, x)
    return l2
```

Alternatively, we can use a `range` with a negative step value, in conjunction with the `append` method. Again, we begin with a fresh, empty list.

```
def reverse(l):
    l2 = []
    for x in range(len(l) - 1, -1, -1):
        l2.append(l[x])
    return l2
```

3

We will use a **for** loop to look at each element, updating two variables to keep track of the smallest and largest numbers seen so far. The important thing to to properly initialise the minimum and maximum variables. We do so by setting them to be equal to the first element of the list. Can you see why?

```
def minmax(l):
    minimum = l[0]
    maximum = l[0]
    for x in l:
        if x < minimum: minimum = x
        if x > maximum: maximum = x
    print('Minimum is ' + str(minimum))
    print('Maximum is ' + str(maximum))
```

This function has a minor inefficiency; it looks at the first element of the list twice. Can you fix that?

4

We need a step value of two, and start and stop values encompassing the whole list:

```
def evens(l):
    return l[0:len(l) + 1:2]
```

Of course, such start and stop values are the default, so we may also write:

```
def evens(l):
    return l[::2]
```

5

We follow the pattern of our second, shorter evens function above, and write simply:

```
def reverse(l):
    return l[::-1]
```

6

We begin by making a fresh, empty list. Then, for each element in the original list, we add it to the new list, unless it is already there:

```
def setify(l):
    l2 = []
    for x in l:
        if x not in l2: l2.append(x)
    return l2
```

7

We use our `setify` function to make a new list of the unique items in the original list. Then we iterate over this new list, finding the number of each of its elements in the original list using the `count` method, and print it.

```
def histogram(l):
    unique = setify(l)
    for x in unique:
        print(str(x) + ' appears ' + str(l.count(x)) + ' times.')
```

8

This is a simple exercise in the use of **in** and the boolean operator **and**:

```
def contains_all(s, a, b, c):
    return a in s and b in s and c in s
```

9

We create a fresh, empty list and append the elements of the original list one by one:

```
def copy_list(l):
    l2 = []
    for x in l: l2.append(x)
    return l2
```

Alternatively, we can use the slice operator with empty start and stop values:

```
def copy_list(l):
    return l[:]
```

10

We make a fresh list with our new `copy_list` function, remove the value using `remove` and then return the new list:

```
def remove_copy(l, x):
    l2 = copy_list(l)
    l2.remove(x)
    return l2
```

11

We set up our alphabet and use list slicing to write a function `rotate` which can rotate it by any number of places from 1 to 25, returning a new string:

```
alphabet = 'ABCDEFGHIJKLMNOPQRSTUVQXYZ'

def rotate(n, a):
    return a[n:] + a[:n]
```

Now our encoding and decoding functions are simple, taking the text to encode or decode, and the rotated cipher. They are, as you would expect, somewhat symmetrical:

```
def encode(text, cipher):
    out = ''
    for x in text:
        if x == ' ': out = out + ' '
        else: out = out + cipher[alphabet.index(x)]
    return out

def decode(text, cipher):
    out = ''
    for x in text:
        if x == ' ': out = out + ' '
        else: out = out + alphabet[cipher.index(x)]
    return out
```

We remember to treat spaces specially.

12

Now that we know about Python's lists, we can dispense with the huge **if** construct of our previous Morse code solution, and work from two lists: the letters and their codes:

```
letters = ['A', 'B', 'C', 'D', 'E', 'F', 'G', 'H',
           'I', 'J', 'K', 'L', 'M', 'N', 'O', 'P',
           'Q', 'R', 'S', 'T', 'U', 'V', 'W', 'X',
           'Y', 'Z', '0', '1', '2', '3', '4', '5',
           '6', '7', '8', '9', '0']

codes = ['. -', '- . . .', '- . - .', '- . .',
         '.', '. . - .', '- - .', '. . . .',
         '. .', '. - - -', '- . -', '. - . .',
         '- -', '- .', '- - -', '. - - .',
         '- - . -', '. - .', '. . .', '-',
         '. . -', '. . . -', '. - -', '- . . -',
         '- . - -', '- - . .', '- - - - -', '. - - - -',
         '. . - - -', '. . . - -', '. . . . -', '- . . . .',
         '- - . . .', '- - - . .', '- - - - .', '- - - - -']
```

Now it is simple to modify our previous solution to look up codes in the list using the `index` method on lists:

```
def print_morse_letter(l):
    if l not in letters: print('bad letter')
    else: print(codes[letters.index(l)], end='   ')

def print_morse(s):
    for l in s:
        if l == ' ': print('    ', end='')
        else: print_morse_letter(l)
    print('')
```

13

First, we shall write a function which looks at a single guess calculates how many are a) the correct number in the correct place and b) the correct number in the incorrect place. This is surprisingly delicate, since we must make sure not to double count anything – for example, if the code is 1441 and the guess is 4444 we should identify two 4s as being correct numbers in the correct places, but the other two 4s are not identified as being correct numbers in the wrong place, because we have already used up all the 4s in our code.

Our function will take two lists of four numbers each, the code and the guess. We copy them, since we will be changing values in the lists to mark them as used. Then we set up two counters, to keep track of how many numbers are correct and in the right place, or correct and in the wrong place.

```
import random

def check_code_guess(code, guess):
    code = code.copy()
    guess = guess.copy()
    correct = 0
    correct_place = 0
    for x in range(0, 4):                    first pass, correct number in correct place
        if guess[x] == code[x]:
            correct = correct + 1
            code[x] = -1                                     mark code as used
            guess[x] = -1                                    mark guess as used
    for x in range(0, 4):
        if guess[x] > -1:
            if guess[x] in code:                        if in remaining code
                correct_place = correct_place + 1
                code[code.index(guess[x])] = -1            mark as used
    print('Correct number in correct place: ' + str(correct))
    print('Correct number in incorrect place: ' + str(correct_place))
    return code == guess
```

The function returns `True` if the code is completely correct, and `False` otherwise. Now we can write the main function which asks the user for a guess repeatedly:

```
def code_guesser():
    a = random.randint(1, 9)                          collect four random digits
    b = random.randint(1, 9)
    c = random.randint(1, 9)
    d = random.randint(1, 9)
    code = [a, b, c, d]
    tries = 1
    i = input()
    guess = [int(i[0]), int(i[1]), int(i[2]), int(i[3])]   extract integers
    while guess != code:
        if check_code_guess(code, guess):
            pass
        else:
            tries = tries + 1
            i = input()
            guess = [int(i[0]), int(i[1]), int(i[2]), int(i[3])]
    print('Correct. You took ' + str(tries) + ' guesses.')
```

There is currently no handling of errors here - what happens if you type in too few or too many numbers, for instance? Can you fix the program to handle this?

Chapter 5 (More with Lists and Strings)

1

We `split` to make a list, then the `sort` method to sort it in place.

```
def sorted_words(s):
    l = s.split()
    l.sort()
    return l
```

2

Using the `sorted` function removes the need to introduce the intermediate name `l` as in the previous question:

```
def sorted_words(s):
    return sorted(s.split())
```

This makes our function a little easier to read.

3

Here is the original from chapter 4:

```
def setify(l):
    l2 = []
    for x in l:
        if x not in l2: l2.append(x)
    return l2

def histogram(l):
    unique = setify(l)
    for x in unique:
        print(str(x) + ' appears ' + str(l.count(x)) + ' times.')
```

The modification is very simple: we use the `sorted` function when creating our list of unique values:

```
def histogram(l):
    unique = sorted(setify(l))
    for x in unique:
        print(str(x) + ' appears ' + str(l.count(x)) + ' times.')
```

4

If we write a function to remove any spaces at the front of a list of strings, we can then use it multiple times to deal with spaces at the beginning and end. Here is such a function:

```python
def strip_leading_spaces(l):
    while len(l) > 0 and l[0] == ' ':
        del l[0]
```

For example, strip_leading_spaces([' ', ' ', 'y', 'e', 's', ' ']) will return ['y', 'e', 's', ' ']. Notice that the **and** operator does not try its right hand side if its left hand side is false. And so, if len(l) > 0 is True, the first element of l will not be tested for equality, and the function succeeds even when the list is empty (or consists only of spaces).

Now we can write the main function, which uses our stripper twice, to remove the spaces at the beginning and end of the list made from the original string. One final reversal brings it back to the correct order, and we join it back into a string.

```python
def remove_spaces(s):
    l = list(s)
    strip_leading_spaces(l)
    l.reverse()
    strip_leading_spaces(l)
    l.reverse()
    return ''.join(l)
```

5

We can (ab)use split and join to make a much simpler definition:

```python
def remove_spaces(s):
    return ' '.join(s.split())
```

This will, however, also remove any excess multiple spaces in between words. Python provides a built-in method strip to remove just the parts at either end, leaving the rest untouched.

6

First, our clip function:

```python
def clip(x):
    if x > 10:
        return 10
    elif x < 1:
        return 1
    else:
        return x
```

Now, we use map with our clip function, not forgetting to use list to get back an ordinary list before returning.

```
def clip_list(l):
    return list(map(clip, l))
```

7

We have already seen how a slice with a step of -1 may be used to reverse a list. A palindrome is something which equals its own reverse, so it is easy to write out the definition:

```
def is_palindromic(s):
    return s == s[::-1]
```

We can use this is_palindromic function as a filter to return only such strings in a list as are palindromic:

```
def palindromes(l):
    return list(filter(is_palindromic, l))
```

Now, we can build only those numbers in a range whose strings are palindromic.

```
def palindromic_numbers_in(x, y):
    ps = palindromes(list(map(str, list(range(x, y)))))
    return list(map(int, ps))
```

We must remember to convert them back to integers before returning. We can achieve this with map, of course. Now we can find all the palindromic numbers up to 500:

```
>>> palindromic_numbers_in(1, 500)
[1, 2, 3, 4, 5, 6, 7, 8, 9, 11, 22, 33, 44, 55, 66, 77, 88, 99, 101, 111, 121,
131,141, 151, 161, 171, 181, 191, 202, 212, 222, 232, 242, 252, 262, 272, 282,
292,303, 313, 323, 333, 343, 353, 363, 373, 383, 393, 404, 414, 424, 434, 444,
454, 464, 474, 484, 494]
```

We can remove the instances of list since range, filter, and map are happy to accept iterators:

```
def is_palindromic(s):
    return s == s[::-1]

def palindromes(l):
    return filter(is_palindromic, l)

def palindromic_numbers_in(x, y):
    ps = palindromes(map(str, range(x, y)))
    return list(map(int, ps))
```

We have to chosen to return an actual list, not a generator, from the final `palindromic_numbers_in` function, however.

8

This is a simple list comprehension, just using `clip` on each item in the list:

```
def clip_list(l):
    return [clip(x) for x in l]
```

9

In this example, we use both **for** and **if** in a list comprehension to process the list of strings.

```
def palindromic_numbers_in(x, y):
    strings = map(str, range(x, y))
    return [int(x) for x in strings if is_palindromic(x)]
```

It is just about readable to put the whole thing in one expression:

```
def palindromic_numbers_in(x, y):
    return [int(x) for x in map(str, range(x, y)) if is_palindromic(x)]
```

Chapter 6 (Prettier Printing)

1

We must keep a counter to prevent the printing of an extra comma and space:

```
def print_list(l):
    length = len(l)
    print('[', end='')
    for x in l:
        print(x, end='')
        length -= 1
        if length > 0: print(', ', end='')
    print(']')
```

This is a lot more complicated than having `print` do the work for us, but it does allow us some customisation: for example if we wished to print without commas, or without spaces.

2

In this instance, format strings do not really help use remove any complexity. In fact, this solution is slightly longer than the one without format strings.

```python
def print_list(l):
    length = len(l)
    print('[', end='')
    for x in l:
        length = length - 1
        if length > 0:
            print(f'{x}, ', end='')
        else:
            print(f'{x}', end='')
    print(']')
```

3

Without format strings, we must use `str` explicitly on each integer, as a prelude to calling the `rjust` method. We can use the `print` function with multiple arguments to print a whole line, though:

```python
def print_powers(n):
    for x in range(1, n):
        x1 = str(x).rjust(5)
        x2 = str(x ** 2).rjust(5)
        x3 = str(x ** 3).rjust(5)
        x4 = str(x ** 4).rjust(5)
        x5 = str(x ** 5).rjust(5)
        print(x1, x2, x3, x4, x5)
```

4

This is a simple substitution of `zfill` for `rjust`:

```python
def print_powers(n):
    for x in range(1, n):
        x1 = str(x).zfill(5)
        x2 = str(x ** 2).zfill(5)
        x3 = str(x ** 3).zfill(5)
        x4 = str(x ** 4).zfill(5)
        x5 = str(x ** 5).zfill(5)
        print(x1, x2, x3, x4, x5)
```

In fact, we can use `rjust(5, '0')` to achieve the same effect.

5

We use the **with** … **as** construct to safely open and close the file. Then it is a matter of carefully constructing the **while** condition and the variable it sets to get the right result. We then rearrange the parts of the name the user types in, and print it to file:

```python
def names_to_file(filename):
    with open(filename, 'w') as f:
        name = 'not empty'
        while name != '':
            name = input('Title, forename and surname, please: ')
            if name != '':
                words = name.split()
                print(words[2], words[1], words[0], sep=', ', file=f)
```

Can you see why we had to initialise the name variable to a non-empty string?

6

Using a format string allows us to remove the sep=', ' argument, but not a lot else:

```python
def names_to_file(filename):
    with open(filename, 'w') as f:
        name = 'not empty'
        while name != '':
            name = input('Title, forename and surname, please: ')
            if name != '':
                words = name.split()
                print(f'{words[2]}, {words[1]}, {words[0]}', file=f)
```

7

For each sentence in the list, we find the position (if any) of the word. Remembering that failure to find the word results in a position of -1, we decide what to print to the screen:

```python
def number_found(sentences, word):
    n = 0
    for s in sentences:
        n += 1
        p = s.find(word)
        if p == -1:
            print(f'{word} not found in sentence {n}')
        else:
            print(f'{word} found at position {p} in sentence {n}')
```

8

This is a simple alteration to the previous answer:

```python
def number_found(sentences, word, filename):
    n = 0
    with open(filename, 'w') as f:
        for s in sentences:
            n += 1
            p = s.find(word)
            if p == -1:
                print(f'{word} not found in sentence {n}', file=f)
            else:
                print(f'{word} found at position {p} in sentence {n}', file=f)
```

Chapter 7 (Arranging Things)

1

This can be achieved by tuple unpacking:

```
Python
>>> a = 1
>>> b = 2
>>> a, b = (b, a)
>>> a
2
>>> b
1
```

Note we do not need parentheses on the tuple when doing multiple assignment of values to names:

```
Python
>>> a = 1
>>> b = 2
>>> a, b = b, a
>>> a
2
>>> b
1
```

However, we cannot write this:

```python
def swap(a, b): a, b = b, a
```

Why not?

2

We can use the `items` method on the dictionary, which allows iterating with a **for** loop using two variables, one for the key and one for the value. We return the result as a tuple.

```python
def unzip(d):
    ks = []
    vs = []
    for k, v in d.items():
        ks.append(k)
        vs.append(v)
    return (ks, vs)
```

For example:

```python
Python
>>> unzip({1: 'one', 2: 'two'})
([1, 2], ['one', 'two'])
```

3

We initialise a fresh, empty dictionary. Then, looping over the index positions in the list of keys, we add each key and its value to the dictionary.

```python
def dict_of_keys_and_values(ks, vs):
    d = {}
    for x in range(0, len(ks)):
        d[ks[x]] = vs[x]
    return d
```

What happens if the lists `ks` and `vs` are of differing lengths?

4

Beginning with an empty dictionary, we loop over the items in each existing dictionary, adding the key and its associated value to the union dictionary.

```python
def union(a, b):
    u = {}
    for x in b: u[x] = b[x]
    for x in a: u[x] = a[x]
    return u
```

The preference for values from dictionary a is achieved by processing it second. Duplicate entries from dictionary b are thus overwritten.

5

The list is being modified by deletion during the **for** loop, and so the indices change. Here is a possible working version, which repeatedly uses the remove method which, we remember, removes the first instance of a given element in a list:

```python
def remove_zeroes(l):
    while 0 in l:
        l.remove(0)
```

6

We need to assign values to two names here, so we use the items method. The rest is then simple:

```python
def reverse_dict(d):
    return {v:k for k, v in d.items()}
```

The output is not always the same length as the input, because a value may appear multiple times in the input, and so be used multiple times as a key in the output:

```python
Python
>>> reverse_dict({1: 2, 2: 1, 3: 1})
{2: 1, 1: 3}
```

7

We remember that an empty set is created by set(). We loop over the input words, using set again to build a set of all the letters in each word, and the | operator to add them to our master set, which we then return:

```python
def letter_set(l):
    letters = set()
    for x in l:
        letters = letters | set(x)
    return letters
```

For example:

```python
Python
>>> letter_set(['one', 'two', 'three'])
{'w', 'n', 't', 'h', 'o', 'r', 'e'}
```

To do the inverse, we shall need a set of all the letters. Then we can use the set difference operator.

```
alphabet = set('qwertyuiopasdfghjklzxcvbnm')

def letters_not_used(l):
    return alphabet - letter_set(l)
```

For example:

```
Python
>>> letters_not_used(['one', 'two', 'three'])
{'m', 'd', 'f', 'q', 'l', 'y', 's', 'k', 'g', 'c', 'v', 'j', 'p', 'a', 'u', 'z',
'x', 'b', 'i'}
```

8

We can represent sets using dictionaries with the values ignored, for example all set to zero. Here is a function to build such a 'set' from a list:

```
def dset_of_list(l):
    s = {}
    for x in l:
        s[x] = 0
    return s
```

Now we can implement the operations. First, for the 'or' operation, we add entries to the new dictionary from both input lists:

```
def dset_or(a, b):
    result = {}
    for x in a: result[x] = 0
    for x in b: result[x] = 0
    return result
```

For 'and', we must check that the item is in both sets:

```
def dset_and(a, b):
    result = {}
    for x in a:
        if x in b:
            result[x] = 0
    return result
```

Set difference is very similar:

```
def dset_minus(a, b):
    result = {}
    for x in a:
        if x not in b:
            result[x] = 0
    return result
```

Finally, exclusive or can be achieved by using our existing functions:

```
def dset_exclusive_or(a, b):
    return dset_or(dset_minus(a, b), dset_minus(b, a))
```

9

We use two **for** portions to iterate over both input sets. Only when x == y do we have a match.

```
def comp_and(a, b):
    return {x for x in a for y in b if x == y}
```

This code checks every possible combination of elements of a and b and so is not very efficient.

10

If the type of the input value t is an integer, we return it. Otherwise, we loop over all the items in t, adding up their sums by recursive application of the sum_all function itself.

```
def sum_all(t):
    if type(t) == int:
        return t
    else:
        total = 0
        for x in t:
            total += sum_all(x)
        return total
```

The result works on any tuple containing only number and on numbers themselves:

```
Python
>>> sum_all((1, 2, 3))
6
>>> sum_all((1, (1, 2), 3))
7
>>> sum_all(10)
10
```

Chapter 8 (When Things Go Wrong)

1

We handle the ValueError resulting from int being used on a string which cannot reasonably be converted to an integer, and ignore the error by using **pass**:

```
def list_sum(l):
    total = 0
    for x in l:
        try:
            total += int(x)
        except ValueError:
            pass
    return total
```

Since the exception is raised by int, the total variable will not be updated in the case of a bad string. So we need not worry about the += operation receiving a bad input.

2

We write two little functions. First, safe_int, which handles the ValueError exception raised by int and returns None instead. Second, the function not_none which returns True if a value is anything other than None. Then we can apply map and filter to build a list of results from safe_int and filter out the None values.

```
def safe_int(s):
    try:
        return int(s)
    except ValueError:
        return None

def not_none(x):
    return x is not None

def list_sum(l):
    return sum(filter(not_none, map(safe_int, l)))
```

3

We handle the ZeroDivisionError exception, returning 0.

```
def safe_division(x, y):
    try:
        return x / y
    except ZeroDivisionError:
        return 0
```

4

We begin with a fresh dictionary. Then, we iterate over the keys and values of dictionary a. We try to insert the corresponding value from b into the new dictionary. If it fails, we handle KeyError and simply skip that key.

```python
def dict_take(a, b):
    c = {}
    for k, v in a.items():
        try:
            c[k] = b[k]
        except KeyError:
            pass
    return c
```

5

It is easy to add all the items from our first dictionary to the new one – the keys are already unique. When we add items from the second, we check to see if the key exists already. If it does, we raise KeyError.

```python
def safe_union(a, b):
    c = {}
    for k, v in a.items():
        c[k] = v
    for k, v in b.items():
        if k in c:
            raise KeyError
        else:
            c[k] = v
    return c
```

6

We check to see if the item is already in the set. If it is, we raise KeyError. If not, we add it as usual.

```python
def add_exception(s, k):
    if k in s:
        raise KeyError
    else:
        s.add(k)
```

Chapter 9 (More with Files)

1

The **with** ... **as** construct allows us to combine the two statements in the original into a single block:

```
with open('gregor.txt') as f:
    for line in f:
        print(line, end='')
```

2

We use **with** ... **as** again, using the optional `file` argument of the `print` function to write each key and value:

```
def dict_to_file(d, filename):
    with open(filename, 'w') as f:
        for k, v in d.items():
            print(k, file=f)
            print(v, file=f)
```

3

This is a good example of the complications of reading from a file, expecting entries in a certain format, and finding data not fitting such a format. We begin with an empty dictionary, and then enter a **while** True loop. We then try to read keys and values, returning if we have reached the end of the file (or if the line is empty).

```
def dict_from_file(filename):
    d = {}
    with open(filename) as f:
        while True:
            try:
                k = f.readline()
                v = f.readline().strip()          to remove newline
                if k !='' and v !='':
                    d[int(k)] = v          int will remove the newline itself
                else:
                    return d
            except ValueError:
                print(f'{k} is not an integer')
```

The `ValueError` exception which may be raised is caught and a message is printed.

4

We open the two input files, and the output file in 'append' mode. Then it is as simple as copying the lines across, being sure not to introduce extra newlines.

```
def append_files(a, b, c):
    with open(a) as f_a, open(b) as f_b, open(c, 'a') as f_c:
        print(f_a.read(), file=f_c, end='')
        print(f_b.read(), file=f_c, end='')
```

5

We use read to get the whole contents of the file at once, split it into 'words', then convert them to integers with map and sum them:

```
def sum_file(filename):
    with open(filename) as f:
        return sum(map(int, f.read().split()))
```

6

This is similar to our append_files function from question 4:

```
def copy_file(a, b):
    with open(a) as f_in, open(b, 'w') as f_out:
        print(f_in.read(), file=f_out, end='')
```

7

We introduce a dictionary to store the character histogram, then create or increment an entry in the dictionary for each character encountered. See page 184 for the program.

8

For the word histogram, we introduce a function clean_split which splits a line into words, then processes each word to remove punctuation, and convert to lowercase. See page 185 for the program.

9

We can reuse clean_split here to get the words in each line. Then, we can use enumerate to iterate over the indices and lists of words for each line. We check for the presence of the search term, and print the line and its number if required. See page 186 for the program.

```
def is_full_stop(s):
    return s == '.'

def stats_from_file(f):
    lines = 0
    characters = 0
    words = 0
    sentences = 0
    histogram = {}
    for line in f:
        lines += 1
        characters += len(line)
        words += len(line.split())
        sentences += len(filter(is_full_stop, line))
        for x in line:
            current = 0
            if x in histogram:             get the current count, if it exists
                current = histogram[x]
            histogram[x] = current + 1
    return (lines, characters, words, sentences, histogram)

def stats_from_filename(filename):
    with open(filename) as f:
        return stats_from_file(f)
```

```python
import string

def clean_split(line):
    return
        [s.strip(string.punctuation).lower() for s in line.split()]

def is_full_stop(s):
    return s == '.'

def stats_from_file(f):
    lines = 0
    characters = 0
    words = 0
    sentences = 0
    histogram = {}
    word_histogram = {}
    for line in f:
        lines += 1
        characters += len(line)
        words += len(line.split())
        sentences += len(filter(is_full_stop, line))
        for x in line:
            current = 0
            if x in histogram:
                current = histogram[x]
            histogram[x] = current + 1
        for x in clean_split(line):
            current = 0
            if x in word_histogram:
                current = word_histogram[x]
            word_histogram[x] = current + 1
    return
        (lines, characters, words, sentences,
         histogram, word_histogram)

def stats_from_filename(filename):
    with open(filename) as f:
        return stats_from_file(f)
```

```
import string

def clean_split(line):
    return
        [s.strip(string.punctuation).lower() for s in line.split()]

def search_word(filename, word):
    lines = []
    with open(filename) as f:
        lines = f.readlines()
    words = map(clean_split, lines)
    for n, ws in enumerate(words):
        if word in ws:
            print(f'{n}: ', end='')
            print(lines[n], end='')
```

10

We read the lines all at once with `readlines`. Then, by careful use of slices, we print five at a time, waiting for the user to press Enter.

```
def top(filename):
    lines = []
    with open(filename) as f:
        lines = f.readlines()
    while len(lines) > 0:
        for l in lines[:5]: print(l, end='')
        lines = lines[5:]
        enter = input()
```

How might this be rewritten to work well on huge files? In that case, reading all the lines at once would be inefficient.

Chapter 10 (The Other Numbers)

1

We calculate the ceiling and floor, and return the closer one, being careful to make sure that a point equally far from the ceiling and floor is rounded up.

```
import math

def round(x):
    c = math.ceil(x)
    f = math.floor(x)
    if c - x <= x - f:
        return c
    else:
        return f
```

2

The function returns another point, and is simple arithmetic.

```
def between(a, b):
    x0, y0 = a
    x1, y1 = b
    return ((x0 + x1) / 2, (y0 + y1) / 2)
```

3

The whole part is calculated using the `floor` function. We return a tuple, the first number being the whole part, the second being the original number minus the whole part. In the case of a negative number, we must be careful – `floor` always rounds downward, not toward zero!

```
import math

def parts(x):
    if x < 0:
        a, b = parts(-x)
        return (-a, b)
    else:
        return (math.floor(x), x - math.floor(x))
```

Notice that we are using the unary operator - to make the number positive.

4

We need to determine at which column the asterisk will be printed. It is important to make sure that the range $0 \ldots 1$ is split into fifty equal sized parts, which requires some careful thought. Then, we just print enough spaces to pad the line, add the asterisk.

```
import math

def star(x):
    i = math.floor(x * 50)
    if i == 50: i = 49
    print(' ' * (i - 1) + '*')
```

5

Our function takes another function as one of its argument. We use a variable to hold the current value, starting at the beginning of the range, and then loop until we are outside the range.

```
def plot(f, a, b, dy):
    pos = a
    while pos <= b:
        star(f(pos))
        pos += dy
```

No allowance has been made here for bad arguments (for example, b smaller than a). Can you extend our program to move the zero-point to the middle of the screen, so that the sine function can be graphed even when its result is less than zero?

Chapter 11 (The Standard Library)

1

Here is the documentation for the `factorial` function from the `math` module.

math.**factorial**(x)

Return x factorial as an integer. Raises `ValueError` if x is not integral or is negative.

We can try it out:

```
Python
>>> import math
>>> math.factorial(5)
120
>>> math.factorial(5.0)
120
>>> math.factorial(-4)
Traceback (most recent call last):
  File "<stdin>", line 1, in <module>
ValueError: factorial() not defined for negative values
```

How does our function differ? Here we have picked the improved factorial function from the questions to chapter 2:

```Python
>>> def factorial(x):
...     if x < 0:
...         return 0
...     elif x == 0:
...         return 1
...     else:
...         return x * factorial(x - 1)
>>> factorial(5)
120
>>> factorial(5.0)
120.0
>>> factorial(-4)
0
```

We return a floating-point number for a floating-point input, unlike `math.factorial`, and we return zero for a negative input, where `math.factorial` raises a `ValueError` exception.

2

We assume the string does represent an integer, then check each potential digit. If it is not in the string `string.digits`, we unset the `is_integer` variable. We then return the variable as the result of the function.

```
import string

def string_is_integer(s):
    is_integer = True
    for x in s:
        if x not in string.digits: is_integer = False
    return is_integer
```

There is one small problem: `string_is_integer('')` will return `True`. Can you fix this?

3

This is a simple modification: we replace the use of `random.randint` with one of `getpass.getpass`, passing the prompt as an argument.

```
import getpass

def guessing_game():
    target = int(getpass.getpass('What is the target number?'))
    guess = int(input('Guess a number between 1 and 100\n'))
    tries = 1
    while guess != target:
        tries += 1
        if guess < target:
            guess = int(input('Higher!\n'))
        elif guess > target:
            guess = int(input('Lower!\n'))
    print(f'Correct! You took {tries} guesses.')
```

4

This is simple. We return them as a tuple.

```
import statistics

def stats(l):
    return
        (statistics.median(l), statistics.mode(l), statistics.mean(l))
```

What happens when there is no modal value in a list?

5

We use two functions: time.sleep, which does nothing for a given number of seconds, allowing us to give the user a count-down; and time.time which returns a floating-point value representing the number of seconds since an arbitrary point in the past. By measuring the time twice, and subtracting, we get the elapsed time.

```
import time

def reaction_test():
    print('Ready? Press Enter when you see ENTER')
    print('3')
    time.sleep(1)
    print('2')
    time.sleep(1)
    print('1')
    time.sleep(1)
    print('ENTER')
    t = time.time()
    enter = input()
    t2 = time.time()
    print(f'Your reaction time was {t2 - t} seconds')
```

What happens if the user presses Enter too soon? Can you fix this?

Chapter 12 (Building Bigger Programs)

1

The guessing_game function is unaltered. We need simply to check that there are enough arguments in sys.argv. If there are, we pass the string representing the maximum number to guessing_game:

```
import getpass
import sys

def guessing_game(maxnum):
    target = int(getpass.getpass('What is the target number?'))
    guess = int(input(f'Guess a number between 1 and {maxnum}\n'))
    tries = 1
    while guess != target:
        tries += 1
        if guess < target:
            guess = int(input('Higher!\n'))
        elif guess > target:
            guess = int(input('Lower!\n'))
    print('Correct! You took {tries} guesses.')

if len(sys.argv) > 1:
    guessing_game(sys.argv[1])
else:
    guessing_game('100')
```

If not, we use the default value of '100'. We could, in fact, pass the number 100 instead of the string '100', since the int function does not care if it is passed something which is already an integer. This, however, would make the program as a whole more difficult to read. Better to keep our types consistent.

2

We first write the file draw.py with our existing plotter:

```
import math

def star(x):
    i = math.floor(x * 50)
    if i == 50: i = 49
    print(' ' * (i - 1) + '*')

def plot(f, a, b, dy):
  pos = a
  while pos <= b:
      star(f(pos))
      pos += dy
```

Now the main plot.py program can use **import** to access the plot function from the draw module, passing the fabricated function f built from the command line argument (one function can sit inside another):

```
import sys
import draw

if len(sys.argv) > 4:
    def f(x): return eval(sys.argv[1])
    draw.plot(f,
                float(sys.argv[2]),
                float(sys.argv[3]),
                float(sys.argv[4]))
else:
    print('Bad arguments')
```

And so we may write:

```
$ python plot.py 'x * x' 0 1 0.1
*
*
  *
    *
      *
        *
          *
            *
              *
                *
                  *
```

What errors might occur? The wrong number of arguments is handled in our program, but what if float fails?

3

We write three little functions to list, add, and remove notes:

```python
import sys

#List notes from a filename, numbered 1..
def list_notes(filename):
    with open(filename, 'r') as f:
        lines = f.readlines()
        for n, l in enumerate(lines):
            print(f'{n + 1}: {l}', end='')

#Append note to the given filename
def add_note(filename, text):
    with open(filename, 'a') as f:
        print(text, file=f)

#Remove note from a filename, given its number.
def remove_note(filename, n):
    with open(filename, 'r') as f_in:
        lines = f_in.readlines()
    with open(filename, 'w') as f_out:
        del lines[n - 1]
        for line in lines:
            f_out.write(line)
```

The main part of the program, then, must decode the command line to decide which operation to do, and what parameters it needs. If the command line too short or malformed, we print a message.

```
#Main
if len(sys.argv) > 1:
    if sys.argv[1] == 'list':
        list_notes(sys.argv[2] + '.txt')
    elif sys.argv[1] == 'remove':
        remove_note(sys.argv[2] + '.txt', int(sys.argv[3]))
    elif sys.argv[1] == 'add':
        add_note(sys.argv[2] + '.txt', sys.argv[3])
    else:
        print('Unrecognized command')
```

Project 1: Pretty Pictures

1

We remember `square` takes the length of the side of the square as an argument:

```
def square(x):
    for _ in range(4):
        t.fd(x)
        t.rt(90)
```

Now we can write `many_squares` which takes how many square to use for the star, and the length of the sides, and calls `square` repeatedly.

```
def many_squares(n, l):
    for _ in range(n):
        square(l)
        t.rt(360.0 / n)
```

2

The `poly` function is unaltered. We define a new function `many_poly` which takes the number of sides, the number of polygons to draw, and the length of the side of each polygon, and calls `poly` repeatedly, turning between each one.

```
def poly(n, l):
    for _ in range(n):
        t.fd(l)
        t.rt(360.0 / n)

def many_poly(sides, number, side_length):
    for _ in range(number):
        poly(sides, side_length)
        t.rt(360.0 / number)
```

Here is the result of many_poly(7, 16, 100):

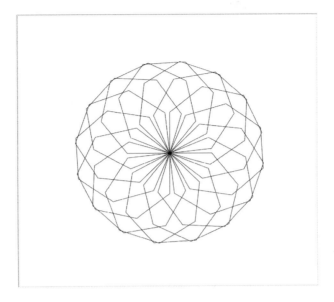

3

The number of segments used to approximate a circle ought to be related to its circumference not its radius.

```
import math

def circle(r):
    circumference = 2.0 * math.pi * r
    poly(int(circumference), 1.0)
```

The smoothness may be fine-tuned by writing int(circumference * 1.5), int(circumference * 0.5) etc.

4

We write a function grid which takes four arguments: the first two to represent the starting point (sx, sy) and the latter two to give the number of circles in the x and y directions:

```
def grid(sx, sy, nx, ny):
    for x in range(nx):
        for y in range(ny):
            t.penup()
            t.goto(sx + x * 50, sy + y * 50)
            t.pendown()
            t.circle(25)
```

Here is the result of `grid(-100, -100, 5, 4)`:

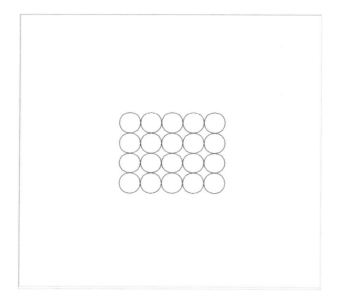

5

There are three dimensions to this data: red, green, and blue. And so we cannot display it directly on a 2D screen – we must flatten it in some way. We have chosen to slice the cube of data into slices based on the red value, and display the slices side by side.

First, we will need a function to draw a filled square of a given size at a given position.

```
def filled_square(x, y, l):
    t.penup()
    t.goto(x, y)
    t.begin_fill()
    t.setheading(90)
    for _ in range(4):
        t.fd(l)
        t.rt(90)
    t.end_fill()
```

Now we write a function `red_gamut` to draw a slice of the cube at a given position for a given red value:

```python
def red_gamut(x, y, r):
    for b in range(11):
        for g in range(11):
            t.color(r, g * 0.1, b * 0.1)
            filled_square(x + b * 5, y + g * 5, 5)
```

Now we can show them side by side.

```python
def whole_gamut():
    for r in range(11):
        red_gamut(-300 + 55 * r, 0, r * 0.1)
```

Here is the result:

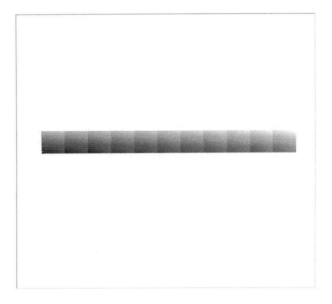

6

Like any other polygon, we simply use `begin_fill` and `end_fill`:

```
import math

def filled_circle(r):
    circumference = 2.0 * math.pi * r
    t.penup()
    t.begin_fill()
    poly(int(circumference), 1.0)
    t.end_fill()
```

Project 1A

Here is one solution – there are, of course, many others. It has two interesting features. The first is a function which returns a function which evaluates the given formula using `eval`. This function may be passed to the graph plotter, and evaluated many times for increasing values of x:

```
def farg(arg):
    def f(x): return eval(arg)
    return f
```

The second is simply a method for cycling through a fixed number of colours in the event that the user wants to plot more graphs than we anticipate. Suppose we have a list of colours of length four:

```
colors = ["black", "red", "green", "blue"]
```

Then we can cycle through them with the % operator:

```
t.pencolor(colors[n % 4])
```

Here is the full program:

```
import sys
import turtle
import math

t = turtle.Turtle()

if len(sys.argv) < 2:
    print('No formula supplied')
    sys.exit(0)

def plot(f):
    t.penup()
    t.goto(-300, f(-300))
    t.pendown()
    for x in range(-300, 300, 1):
        t.goto(x, f(x))
```

```python
def farg(arg):
    def f(x): return eval(arg)
    return f

def key(n, formula_text, color):
    t.color(color)
    t.penup()
    t.goto(-300, -200 - 20 * n)
    t.pendown()
    t.write(formula_text, font = ("Arial", 16, "normal"))

def line(x0, y0, x1, y1):
    t.penup()
    t.goto(x0, y0)
    t.pendown()
    t.goto(x1, y1)

def axes():
    t.color("black")
    line(-300, 0, 300, 0)
    line(0, -300, 0, 300)
    for x in range(-300, 301, 50):
        if x != 0:
            t.penup()
            t.goto(x, -20)
            t.pendown()
            t.write(str(x), font = ("Arial", 12, "normal"))
            line(x, -5, x, 5)
    for y in range(-300, 301, 50):
        if y != 0:
            t.penup()
            t.goto(-20, y)
            t.pendown()
            t.write(str(y), font = ("Arial", 12, "normal"))
            line(-5, y, 5, y)

colors = ["black", "red", "green", "blue"]

t.speed(0)

axes()

for n, arg in enumerate(sys.argv[1:]):
    t.pencolor(colors[n % 4])
    plot(farg(arg))
    key(n, arg, colors[n % 4])

turtle.mainloop()
```

PROJECT 1B

A clock face is a good example of a structure which is easier to produce with turtle-like commands than by calculating coordinates and using goto.

The main loop checks the time, clears the screen, and then draws the clock face. Then we use turtle.Screen().update to update the screen, and sleep for one second:

```python
while True:
    tm = time.localtime()
    t.home()
    t.clear()
    clockface(tm.tm_hour, tm.tm_min, tm.tm_sec)
    turtle.Screen().update()
    time.sleep(1)
```

Here is the full program:

```python
import turtle
import time

def hand(length, thickness, angle):
    t.penup()
    t.home()
    t.setheading(90)
    t.pensize(thickness)
    t.pendown()
    t.rt(angle)
    t.fd(length)

def tickmarks():
    t.pensize(1)
    for a in range (0, 60):
        t.penup()
        t.home()
        t.setheading(90)
        t.rt(360 / 60 * a)
        t.fd(295)
        t.pendown()
        t.fd(5)

def clockface(h, m, s):
    t.penup()
    t.goto(0, -300)
    t.pensize(1)
    t.pendown()
    t.circle(300)
    tickmarks()
    hand(200, 3, 360 / 12 * (h % 12))
```

```
    hand(280, 3, 360 / 60 * m)
    hand(295, 1, 360 / 60 * s)

t = turtle.Turtle()
t.hideturtle()
turtle.Screen().tracer(0, 0)

while True:
    tm = time.localtime()
    t.home()
    t.clear()
    clockface(tm.tm_hour, tm.tm_min, tm.tm_sec)
    turtle.Screen().update()
    time.sleep(1)
```

Project 2: Counting Calories

1

We use the function os.path.join to combine the person's name and the name of the file where we expect to find the weights listed, and load the table with table_of_file. We can then iterate over the resultant table with the items method:

```
def list_weights(name):
    for k, vs in table_of_file(os.path.join(name, 'weight.txt')).items():
        print(f'{k} {vs[0]}')
```

Printing the dates and weights to the screen is then simple.

2

We use the suggested os.listdir function to get the list of filenames. We are not told anything about the order, so we sort it with sorted – owing to the format for dates which we have chosen, they sort correctly.

```
def list_dates(name):
    for filename in sorted(os.listdir(name)):
        if filename != 'weight.txt': print(filename[:-4])
```

We must exclude the weight.txt file, of course.

3

We must take account of the possibility that no weight was recorded for a given date. In this case, the table lookup will yield None.

```
def lookup_weight(name, date):
    table = table_of_file(os.path.join(name, 'weight.txt'))
    vs = table[date]
    if vs is None:
        print(f'No weight found for {date}')
    elif len(vs) > 0:
        print(f'Weight at {date} was {vs[0]}')
```

4

We make the new directory, then open a file in it. The file is created, even though we do not write anything to it.

```
def new_user(name):
    os.mkdir(name)
    with open(os.path.join(name, 'weight.txt'), 'w'):
        pass
```

6

Here is the full csvcals.py program:

```
import sys
import os
import datetime
import csv

def table_of_file(filename):
    with open(filename) as c:
        r = csv.reader(c)
        next(r)
        table = {}
        for row in r:
            table[row[0]] = row[1:]
        return table

def list_eaten(name, date):
    for k, vs in table_of_file(os.path.join(name, date) + '.csv').items():
        print(f'{k} {vs[0]}')

def list_weights(name):
```

```
        for k, vs in table_of_file(os.path.join(name, 'weight.csv')).items():
            print(f'{k} {vs[0]}')

def list_dates(name):
    for filename in sorted(os.listdir(name)):
        if filename != 'weight.csv': print(filename[:-4])

def list_foods():
    for k, vs in table_of_file('calories.csv').items():
        print(k, end=' ')
        for v in vs: print(v, end=' ')
        print('')

def lookup_calories(food):
    table = table_of_file('calories.csv')
    vs = table[food]
    if vs is None:
        print(f'Food {food} not found')
    else:
        if len(vs) > 1:
            weight = vs[0]
            calories = vs[1]
            print(f'There are {calories} calories in {weight}g of {food}')
        else:
            print(f'Malformed calorie entry for {food} in calories file')

def lookup_weight(name, date):
    table = table_of_file(os.path.join(name, 'weight.csv'))
    vs = table[date]
    if vs is None:
        print(f'No weight found for {date}')
    elif len(vs) > 0:
        print(f'Weight at {date} was {vs[0]}')

def total_date(name, date):
    calories = table_of_file('calories.csv')
    table = table_of_file(os.path.join(name, date) + '.csv')
    total = 0
    for k, vs in table.items():
        weight_and_calories = calories[k]
        reference_weight = int(weight_and_calories[0])
        reference_calories = int(weight_and_calories[1])
        calories_per_gram = reference_calories / reference_weight
        total += int(vs[0]) * calories_per_gram
    print(f'Total calories for {date}: {int(total)}')

def new_user(name):
    os.mkdir(name)
```

```
    with open(os.path.join(name, 'weight.csv'), 'w') as f:
        print('Date,Weight', file=f)

def date_today():
    d = datetime.datetime.now()
    return f'{d.day:02}-{d.month:02}-{d.year}'

def eaten(name, food, grams):
    filename = os.path.join(name, date_today()) + '.csv'
    is_new = not os.path.exists(filename)
    with open(filename, 'a') as f:
        if is_new: print('Food,Weight', file=f)
        print(f'"{food}",{grams}', file=f)

def weighed(name, weight):
    filename = os.path.join(name, 'weight.csv')
    is_new = not os.path.exists(filename)
    with open(filename, 'a') as f:
        if is_new: print('Date,Weight', file=f)
        print(f'{date_today()},{weight}', file=f)

arg = sys.argv

if len(arg) > 1:
    cmd = arg[1]
    if cmd == 'list':
        if len(arg) > 3 and arg[2] == 'eaten':
            list_eaten(arg[3], arg[4])
        else:
            if arg[2] == 'weights' and len(arg) > 3:
                list_weights(arg[3])
            elif arg[2] == 'dates' and len(arg) > 3:
                list_dates(arg[3])
            elif arg[2] == 'foods':
                list_foods()
    elif cmd == 'lookup':
        if len(arg) > 2:
            if arg[2] == 'calories':
                lookup_calories(arg[3])
            elif arg[2] == 'weight' and len(arg) > 3:
                lookup_weight(arg[3], arg[4])
    elif cmd == 'total':
        if len(arg) > 3:
            total_date(arg[2], arg[3])
    elif cmd == 'newuser':
        if len(arg) > 2:
            new_user(arg[2])
    elif cmd == 'eaten':
```

```
    if len(arg) > 4:
        eaten(arg[2], arg[3], arg[4])
elif cmd == 'weighed':
    if len(arg) > 3:
        weighed(arg[2], arg[3])
else:
    print('Command not understood')
```

7

There are only two functions to change: those that write non-blank CSV files. We use `csv.writer` to create a CSV writer from the file, then the `writerow` method to write both column headers and data.

```
def eaten(name, food, grams):
    filename = os.path.join(name, date_today()) + '.csv'
    is_new = not os.path.exists(filename)
    with open(filename, 'a') as f:
        w = csv.writer(f)
        if is_new: w.writerow(['Food', 'Weight'])
        w.writerow([food, grams])

def weighed(name, weight):
    filename = os.path.join(name, 'weight.csv')
    is_new = not os.path.exists(filename)
    with open(filename, 'a') as f:
        w = csv.writer(f)
        if is_new: w.writerow(['Date', 'Weight'])
        w.writerow([date_today(), weight])
```

Project 3: Noughts and Crosses

1

A 1x1 game is always won by the first player to play on their first turn. A 2x2 game is always won by the first player to play on their second turn. In some sense, of course, 3x3 is not interesting either because, as every child finds out soon enough, a draw can always be forced. What happens with a 4x4 game?

2

The most important rules are winning when one can, and blocking the other player if they are about to win. When not in either of those situations, you might think about which spaces are better to hold, for example the centre square.

3

To make a random play, we can choose a number between zero and eight. If the space is blank, we play there. If not, we cycle around the positions until we find a blank one.

```
def random_play(pl, b):
    p = random.randint(0, 8)
    while b[p] != '_':
        p = (p + 1) % 9
    b[p] = pl
```

The function assumes that there is always at least one blank space to find. Now the random_game function is straightforward:

```
def random_game():
    b = emptyboard.copy()
    pl = 'O'
    while not (full(b) or wins('X', b) or wins('O', b)):
        print_board(b)
        print('')
        random_play(pl, b)
        if pl == 'O': pl = 'X'
        else: pl = 'O'
    print_board(b)
    print('Game over. Result:')
    if wins('O', b):
        print('O wins!')
    elif wins('X', b):
        print('X wins!')
    else:
        print('Draw!')
```

4

We ask for input from the user, in the form of a string. First, we check that it represents a digit, to avoid an error when using int. Then we check it is in range. Finally, we check the space is really blank. Only then can we make the move.

```
def human_move(board):
    n_input = input('Position 0..8? ')
    if n_input.isdigit():
        n = int(n_input)
        if n < 0 or n > 8:
            print('Board position must be from 0..8')
            human_move(board)
        else:
            if board[n] != '_':
                print('Position already taken')
                human_move(board)
            else:
                board[n] = 'O'
    else:
        print('Not a valid board position')
```

This function can also be written without recursion, with the use of a **while** loop.

5

Extending the human_move function is simple: we add an extra argument.

```
def human_move(pl, board):
    n_input = input('Position 0..8? ')
    if n_input.isdigit():
        n = int(n_input)
        if n < 0 or n > 8:
            print('Board position must be from 0..8')
            human_move(pl, board)
        else:
            if board[n] != '_':
                print('Position already taken')
                human_move(pl, board)
            else:
                board[n] = pl
    else:
        print('Not a valid board position')
        human_move(pl, board)
```

There are many ways we might choose to write the main play function. Here is one:

```
def play():
    pl = 'X'
    print('Board is numbered\n012\n345\n678\n')
    board = emptyboard.copy()
    while not (full(board) or wins('X', board) or wins('O', board)):
        print(f'Player {pl} to play...')
        human_move(pl, board)
        if pl == 'X':
            pl = 'O'
        else:
            pl = 'X'
        print_board(board)
    print('Game over. Result:')
    if wins('O', board):
        print('You win!')
    elif wins('X', board):
        print('Computer wins!')
    else:
        print('Draw!')
```

6

The empty corner and empty side tactics are simple (the order we search for a blank space does not matter):

```
def tactic_empty_corner(b):
    return try_to_take(b, [0, 2, 6, 8])

def tactic_empty_side(b):
    return try_to_take(b, [1, 3, 5, 7])
```

This tactic requires us to check that the opposite corner has been taken by the opposing side, so a single call to try_to_take cannot suffice.

```
def tactic_play_opposite_corner(b):
    if b[0] == 'X':
        if try_to_take(b, [8]): return True
    elif b[2] == 'X':
        if try_to_take(b, [6]): return True
    elif b[6] == 'X':
        if try_to_take(b, [2]): return True
    elif b[8] == 'X':
        return try_to_take(b, 0)
```

We can update the computer_move function, adding these three new tactics and removing our earlier tactic_first_blank, since the combination of the centre, empty corner and empty side tactics render it unused.

```
def computer_move(b):
    print('Computer has played:')
    if tactic_win(b):
        print('Used tactic_win')
        return
    if tactic_block(b):
        print('Used tactic_block')
        return
    if tactic_play_centre(b):
        print('Used tactic_centre')
        return
    if tactic_play_opposite_corner(b):
        print('Used tactic_play_opposite_corner')
        return
    if tactic_empty_corner(b):
        print('Used tactic_empty_corner')
        return
    if tactic_empty_side(b):
        print('Used tactic_empty_side')
        return
    print('No tactic applied: error in tactic implementations')
```

7

One solution is overleaf. The boolean human_goes_first is true if the human player moves first.

8

The fork tactic requires us to look at each pair of intersecting lines, trying to find two such lines each of which have one of our pieces and two blank spaces. If we find such a pair, and if the intersecting space is blank, we play it. Otherwise, the tactic fails. So we shall need a list of the pairs of intersecting lines in a board, together with the space at which they intersect:

```
intersecting_lines = [(h1, v1, 0), (h1, v2, 1), (h1, v3, 2),
                       (h2, v1, 3), (h2, v2, 4), (h2, v3, 5),
                       (h3, v1, 6), (h3, v2, 7), (h3, v3, 8),
                       (d1, h1, 0), (d1, h2, 4), (d1, h3, 8),
                       (d1, v1, 0), (d1, v2, 4), (d1, v3, 8),
                       (d2, h1, 2), (d2, h2, 4), (d2, h3, 6),
                       (d2, v1, 2), (d2, v2, 4), (d2, v3, 6),
                       (d1, d2, 4)]
```

Now for the fork tactic itself, we go through the pairs of intersecting lines. For each one, we look up those positions on the board. Then we can check the count of pieces in each, and check that the intersecting space is blank. If so, we make the play. If not, we return False.

```
def play(human_goes_first):
    print('Board is numbered\n012\n345\n678\n')
    board = emptyboard.copy()
    if human_goes_first:
        print('You go first...')
        print_board(board)
    else:
        print('Computer goes first...')
    while not (full(board) or wins('X', board) or wins('O', board)):
        if human_goes_first:
            human_move(board)
        else:
            computer_move(board)
        human_goes_first = not human_goes_first
        print_board(board)
    print('Game over. Result:')
    if wins('O', board):
        print('You win!')
    elif wins('X', board):
        print('Computer wins!')
    else:
        print('Draw!')
```

```
def tactic_fork(b):
    for (l, l2, i) in intersecting_lines:
        bl = [b[x] for x in l]
        bl2 = [b[x] for x in l2]
        l_fits = bl.count('_') == 2 and bl.count('X') == 1
        l2_fits = bl2.count('_') == 2 and bl2.count('X') == 1
        if l_fits and l2_fits and b[i] == '_':
            b[i] = 'X'
            return True
    return False
```

The block fork tactic is somewhat more complicated. Part of the condition (two intersecting lines with one opponent's piece and two blanks) is similar to the fork tactic, but we do not necessarily move to the intersection space, even if it is blank. First, we check to find a place to move which makes two of our pieces in a row. If so, we take it instead, forcing our opponent to block instead of fork.

The function find_two_in_a_row, given a board and a position, checks to see if the position, if taken, would make us two in a row. If so, we take it.

```
def find_two_in_row(b, p):
    if b[p] == '_':
        for l in lines:
            if p in l:
                bl = [b[x] for x in l]
                if bl.count('X') == 1 and bl.count('O') == 0:
                    b[p] = 'X'
                    return True
    else:
        return False
```

Now the main function checks the initial conditions, calls two_in_a_row as required and, should it fail each time, deals with the case of the intersecting space:

```
def tactic_block_fork(b):
    for (l, l2, i) in intersecting_lines:
        bl = [b[x] for x in l]
        bl2 = [b[x] for x in l2]
        l_fits = bl.count('_') == 2 and bl.count('O') == 1
        l2_fits = bl2.count('_') == 2 and bl2.count('O') == 1
        if l_fits and l2_fits and b[i] == '_':
            if find_two_in_row(b, l[0]): return True
            elif find_two_in_row(b, l[1]): return True
            elif find_two_in_row(b, l[2]): return True
            elif find_two_in_row(b, l2[0]): return True
            elif find_two_in_row(b, l2[1]): return True
            elif find_two_in_row(b, l2[2]): return True
            else:
                if b[i] == '_':
                    b[i] = 'X'
                    return True
    return False
```

Here is the complete computer_move function for all our tactics, including printing each one out if it is applied, for debugging purposes:

```
def computer_move(b):
    print('Computer has played:')
    if tactic_win(b):
        print('Used tactic_win')
        return
    if tactic_block(b):
        print('Used tactic_block')
        return
    if tactic_fork(b):
        print('Used tactic_fork')
        return
    if tactic_block_fork(b):
        print('Used tactic_block_fork')
        return
    if tactic_play_centre(b):
        print('Used tactic_centre')
        return
    if tactic_play_opposite_corner(b):
        print('Used tactic_play_opposite_corner')
        return
    if tactic_empty_corner(b):
        print('Used tactic_empty_corner')
        return
    if tactic_empty_side(b):
        print('Used tactic_empty_side')
        return
    print('No tactic applied: error in tactic implementations')
```

9

O wins 77904 times, calculated by a similar function to the one we used to find how many times X wins:

```
def sum_o_wins(t):
    b, bs = t
    ns = wins('O', b)
    for board in bs:
        ns += sum_o_wins(board)
    return ns

o_wins = sum_o_wins(x_game_tree)
```

The number of drawn games is 46080 can be calculated similarly, counting one for each board in the tree which is full but not won by any player:

```
def drawn_games(t):
    b, bs = t
    ns = wins('X', b) and not wins('O', b) and full(b)
    for board in bs:
        ns += drawn_games(board)
    return ns

drawn = drawn_games(x_game_tree)
```

To calculate the total number of games, we can look for all boards which are full or won. This comes to 255168.

```
def num_games(t):
    b, bs = t
    ns = wins('O', b) or wins('X', b) or full(b)
    for board in bs:
        ns += num_games(board)
    return ns

games = num_games(x_game_tree)
```

Another way to find all boards which are full or won is to look for boards with no sub-trees.

Of course, we need only find two of the three outcomes of a game – we can deduce the third by subtraction from the total number of games.

10

We write a function traverses the tree, counting one for each time the function passed to it returns True.

```
def sum_game_tree(f, t):
    b, bs = t
    ns = f(b)
    for sb in bs:
        ns += sum_game_tree(f, sb)
    return ns
```

Now, we can write simple little functions to pass to sum_game_tree:

```
x_game_tree = game_tree('X')

def f(b): return wins('X', b)
x_wins = sum_game_tree(f, x_game_tree)

def f(b): return wins('O', b)
o_wins = sum_game_tree(f, x_game_tree)

def f(b): return not wins('X', b) and not wins('O', b) and full(b)
draw = sum_game_tree(f, x_game_tree)

def f(b): return wins('X', b) or wins('O', b) or full(b)
games = sum_game_tree(f, x_game_tree)
```

11

We can write the tree out using nested tuples, each consisting of three elements: the current node, the left branch and the right branch. We use '?' for nodes which do not correspond to a valid letter or number:

```
tree = ('?',
        ('E',
            ('I',
                ('S',
                    ('H', '5', '4'),
                    ('V', '?', '3')),
                ('U',
                    'F',
                    ('?', '?', '2'))),
            ('A',
                ('R', 'L', '?'),
                ('W', 'P',
                    ('J', '?', '1')))),
        ('T',
            ('N',
                ('D',
                    ('B', '6', '?'), 'X'),
                ('K', 'C', 'Y')),
            ('M',
                ('G',
                    ('Z', '7', '?'), 'Q'),
                ('O',
                    ('?', '8', '?'), ('?', '9', '0')))))
```

Now we need a function to look through a given code, and traverse the tree, going left for each dot and right for each dash. When we have finished, we check to see if we have a string or a tuple and extract the string if we need to.

```
def decode_morse(code):
    t = tree
    for c in code:
        if c == ' ':
            pass
        elif c == '.':
            n, l, r = t
            t = l
        else:
            n, l, r = t
            t = r
    if type(t) == tuple:
        n, l, r = t
        return n
    else:
        return t
```

Now we must write a function to split a string into individual codes, recognising seven spaces as one space in the output:

```
def split_string(string):
    codes = []                                              output codes
    spaces = 0                                   spaces in current run of spaces
    code = ''                                               current code
    for c in string:
        if c == ' ':
            if code != '' and spaces > 0:
                codes.append(code)                          completed code
                code = ''
            spaces = spaces + 1
        else:
            if spaces == 7: codes.append(' ')               word space found
            spaces = 0
            code = code + c
    if code != '': codes.append(code)
    return codes
```

Now the main function is simple: we use `split_string` to get a list of codes, including the spaces we have found, and decode each non-Space code and print it:

```
def decode_morse_string(string):
    for code in split_string(string):
        if code == ' ': print(' ', end='')
        else: print(decode_morse(code), end='')
    print('')
```

Project 4: Photo Finish

1

We will design appropriate functions for brightness and contrast, and then test them on our image.

For some combinations of brightness and contrast factors and pixel values, these functions will return values less than 0 or more than 255. We begin, then, with a function `clamp` to make sure that does not happen, and the resulting pixel value is in range:

```
def clamp(x):
    if x < 0: return 0
    elif x > 255: return 255
    else: return x
```

There is no right or wrong formula for brightness or contrast. Here, we have chosen to take brightness values expected to be generally from -2 to 2, -2 meaning very dim, 2 meaning very bright:

```
def brightness(p, x):
    r, g, b = p
    r_out = clamp(int(r + x * 128))
    g_out = clamp(int(g + x * 128))
    b_out = clamp(int(b + x * 128))
    return (r_out, g_out, b_out)
```

For contrast, we use simple multiplication. This assumes inputs of 0 upwards.

```
def contrast(p, x):
    r, g, b = p
    r_out = clamp(int(r * x))
    g_out = clamp(int(g * x))
    b_out = clamp(int(b * x))
    return (r_out, g_out, b_out)
```

Now we can define functions to perform our operation on a whole image, using the `process_pixels` function we wrote earlier:

```
def brightness_image(i, x):
    def b(p): return brightness(p, x)
    return process_pixels(b, i)

def contrast_image(i, x):
    def c(p): return contrast(p, x)
    return process_pixels(c, i)
```

Now we can use these functions with some test values for brightness and contrast, and save them.

```
bright = brightness_image(i, 0.5)
dim = brightness_image(i, -0.5)
low_contrast = contrast_image(i, 0.25)
high_contrast = contrast_image(i, 1.5)

bright.save('bright.png')
dim.save('dim.png')
low_contrast.save('low_contrast.png')
high_contrast.save('high_contrast.png')
```

Here are the results. They are, from right to left: `bright.png`, `dim.png`, `low_contrast.png`, and `high_contrast.png`:

2

To flip horizontally, we range over the left hand half of the image, swapping pixels with the equivalents on the right hand side.

```
def hflip(i):
    p = i.load()
    sx, sy = i.size
    for x in range(sx // 2):
        for y in range(sy):
            r = p[x, y]
            p[x, y] = p[sx - x - 1, y]
            p[sx - x - 1, y] = r
```

If the image has an odd width, the middle column is not touched. This is a consequence of the rounding-down behaviour of the `//` operator. A similar function can be written for the vertical flip:

```
def vflip(i):
    p = i.load()
    sx, sy = i.size
    for y in range(sy // 2):
        for x in range(sx):
            r = p[x, y]
            p[x, y] = p[x, sy - y - 1]
            p[x, sy - y - 1] = r
```

Rotation by 180 degrees is a simple combination of the two (try it with a piece of paper you have marked the corners of):

```
def rotate180(i):
    hflip(i)
    vflip(i)
```

3

The changes are simple:

```
def blur_in_place(i):
    p = i.load()
    sx, sy = i.size
    for x in range(3, sx - 3):
        for y in range(3, sy - 3):
            sumr, sumg, sumb = 0, 0, 0
            for dx in range(-1, 2):
                for dy in range(-1, 2):
                    sourcer, sourceg, sourceb = p[x + dx, y + dy]
                    sumr = sumr + sourcer
                    sumg = sumg + sourceg
                    sumb = sumb + sourceb
            p[x, y] = (int(sumr / 9), int(sumg / 9), int(sumb / 9))
```

We can test by blurring three times, just like we did with our original blur function. The new (right) and old (left) results are similar but not the same – the in-place blur is blurrier.

4

We need a border of width 1 for each blur operation, to avoid losing content over the edge:

```
def blur_auto(i, n):
    i = border(i, n, (255, 255, 255))
    for x in range(n):
        i = blur(i)
    return i
```

5

This is simple enough – and you could extend it to add a border too.

```
i = Image.open('rabbit.png')

images = [i]

for x in range(99):
    i = blur(i)
    images.append(i)

images[0].save('blur.gif', save_all=True, append_images=images[1:],
               duration=100, loop=0)
```

Here is frame 100:

Hints for Questions

Chapter 1
Starting Off

1

Try to work these out on paper, and then check by typing them in. Can you show possible steps of evaluation for each expression?

2

Type it in. What does Python print? Consider the precedence of + and *.

Chapter 2
Names and Functions

2

What does the function take as arguments? You can use the != operator and the **and** keyword here.

3

The function will have three arguments i.e. **def** volume(w, h, d): ...

4

Can you define this in terms of the is_vowel function we have already written?

5

When does it not terminate? Can you add a check to see when it might happen, and return 0 instead? What is the factorial of 0 anyway?

6

What is the sum of all the integers from 1 ... 1? Perhaps this is a good start.

7

What happens when you raise a number to the power 0? What about the power 1? What about a higher power?

8

You can use an additional argument to keep track of which number the function is going to try to divide by.

Chapter 3
Again and Again

1

Make sure to consider how the start and stop arguments are defined at the beginning of this chapter.

3

You will need a local variable to store the count.

6

The `input` function with an argument, and using the \n newline sequence might look like this:

```
entered =
    input('Please enter the password\n')
```

To remove the `entered` variable, we can do the `input` inside the **while** loop's test itself.

7

You might need three variables: the chosen secret number, the current guess, and the number of tries so far. Remember the `int` function can convert a string to an integer.

8

This is just a big **if** construct. Make sure not to output both a letter space and a word space at the end of a word – just a word space.

Chapter 4
Making Lists

2

Try making a fresh, empty list, and then putting items from the original list into it one by one.

Maybe you could use the `insert` method to put them in a particular place.

3

What initial value can we use for keeping track of both the maximum number seen and the minimum number seen?

6

Start from a fresh, empty list. Then, looking at each element of the original list, decide whether it should go into the new list or not.

7

You can use the `setify` function you have already written to find the unique items, and then the `count` method to find out how many of each appear in the input list.

11

The rotation may be achieved by slicing.

13

The problem may be split into two. First identify "correct numbers in the correct place" then "correct numbers in incorrect place". In the latter stage, be careful not to use any position in the code identified in the first stage, nor to use a position twice.

Chapter 5
More with Lists and Strings

1

We already know how to make the list of words with `split`.

4

Just a function to remove spaces from the beginning of a list is required; the rest can be done with list reversal.

9

Remember that a list comprehension can have an **if** part as well as a **for** part.

Chapter 6
Prettier Printing

1

Remember not to add a comma or space after the final item. We did this once before, in chapter 3 question 4.

3

Recall that `print` can take multiple values.

5

How will the user signal that they have no more names to type in?

Chapter 7
Arranging Things

1

Remember that we can assign to a tuple using tuple unpacking: `a, b = ...`

2

The `items` method, described in the chapter, can be used to iterate on two variables at once with **for** k, v = ...

5

Consider the indices when deletion happens.

6

The `items` method, described in the chapter can be used to iterate on two variables at once with **for** k, v = ...

7

Remember that `set` can build a set of the letters in a string.

Chapter 8
When Things Go Wrong

2

The technique is to use map to build a list (possibly containing `None` values), then filter it to remove them.

Chapter 9
More with Files

3

What happens if `int` cannot proceed because the file is malformed? How will you know when all the entries have been read?

5

The `split` method works, of course, equally well on numbers as on words.

7

A dictionary is suitable for storing a histogram. When do we need to add a new entry? When do we need to increment an existing entry?

Chapter 10
The Other Numbers

1

Consider the two functions `math.ceil` and `math.floor`.

3

Consider the function `math.floor`. What should happen in the case of a negative number?

4

Calculate the column number for the asterisk carefully. How can it be printed in the correct column?

5

You will need to call the `star` function with an appropriate argument at points between the beginning and end of the range, as determined by the step.

Chapter 11
The Standard Library

2

The string `string.digits` is `'0123456789'`.

5

The use of `time.sleep` is to provide a count-down for the user.

Chapter 12
Building Bigger Programs

1

The two cases (a maximum is provided, and is not provided) may be distinguished by testing the length of the `sys.argv` list.

2

The `plot` function requires a function to be passed to it. We can build such a function from the argument provided on the command line, using the `eval` function.

Project 1: Pretty Pictures

3

The number of segments used to approximate a circle ought to be related to its circumference not its radius.

5

There are three dimensions to the gamut: red, green and blue. Since we cannot display these on a 2D screen, you must find a way to 'flatten' the space out.

PROJECT 1A

We need to build a function which can be called repeatedly to evaluate an expression from the command line, in terms of x. Can you write a function to return such a function?

PROJECT 1B

Recall that `turtle.Screen().tracer(0, 0)` turns off animation, and that you will need `turtle.Screen().update()` to show the clock face when you have finished drawing it, and that `time.sleep` may be used to wait for the next time we need to draw a clock.

Project 2: Counting Calories

1

Remember that the `items` method may be used to iterate over the keys and values of the table resulting from `table_of_file`.

2

The dates will sort as if they were in alphabetical order – the digits too are ordered.

3

If a table lookup fails, `None` is returned.

Project 3: Noughts and Crosses

3

The `random_move` function will need a mechanism to pick a random blank space. You might repeatedly pick spaces until one is found to be blank, though this may be inefficient when few spaces remain.

Another way would be to pick a random place to start, and then cycle through the positions in turn until a blank one is found.

6

Our `try_to_take` function is useful here.

8

Draw out diagrams of the situations described by the rules. You will need a list of intersecting lines and the points at which they intersect.

9

To calculate the total number of boards, remember only to count ones which are full or won.

10

The function must traverse the whole tree, counting once for each board for which the function passed to it returns `True`.

11

The tree may be represented by nested tuples of three items each, representing the data, the left branch and the right branch.

Project 4: Photo Finish

1

There is no right or wrong answer for the formulae for brightness and contrast. Design them to produce a sensible result for a sensible input.

2

Rotation may be achieved by a combination of flips.

4

Consider how the blurring operation spreads the colour of a pixel around: how do we make sure we lose none?

Index

*, 3, 25
+, 3, 14, 36
-, 3, 68
<, 3
<=, 3
==, 3
>, 3
>=, 3
%, 7
&, 68
^, 68
__pycache__, 21

and, 4
append, 36
argument, 12
as, 58
atan, 98

boolean, 3

ceil, 98
comparison operator, 3
copy, 38
cos, 98
count, 38
Ctrl-C, ix

def, 12
del, 37
dictionary, 65
    deleting from, 66
    iterating over, 66
division by zero, 95

elif, 14
else, 13

empty list, 33
enumerate, 35
EOFError, 77
except, 77
exception, 77
    when reading a file, 88
exit(), ix
expression, 1

factorial, 15
False, 3
file, 58
    exceptions, 88
    reading from, 85
FileNotFoundError, 77
filter, 48
find, 46
float, 97
floating-point, 95
    number, 95
    repeated calculation
        with, 100
floor, 98
for ... **in** ..., 23
for loop
    inside another, 24
    over a string, 25
format string, 56
from ... **import** ..., 21
function, 12
    of multiple arguments,
        14
    recursive, 15
    spanning multiple
        lines, 12

get, 76

if, 13
immutability, 37
import, 21
in, 66
indentation, 13
index, 38
IndexError, 77
input, 26
insert, 37
int, 28, 97
integer, 2
items, 66
iterate, 25
    over dictionary, 66

join, 45

key, dictionary, 65
KeyError, 77
keyword, 12

len, 25
list, 33
    appending to, 36
    comprehension, 49
    copying, 38
    empty, 33
    iterating over, 34
    membership of, 38
    pop from, 37
    sort, 47
list, 34, 40
list comprehension, 49
log, 98
log10, 98
lower, 91

map, 48
math, 98
max, 56
min, 56
module, 105
modulus, 7
mutability, 37

name, 11
    global, 27
    local, 27
NameError, 77
None, 75
not in, 66
number, 2
    floating-point, 95
    integer, 2
    real, 95
    whole, 2

operator
    arithmetic, 3
    comparison, 3
or, 4

pass, 29
pop, 37
print, 1
    to a file, 58
    with separator, 55
print, 1
program, ix
programming language, ix

Python, ix
    .py file, 21
    script, 21
    Standard Library, 105
    version numbers, ix

raise, 78
random, 30
range, 23
read, 85
readline, 86
readlines, 89
real number, 95
recursive function, 15
remainder, 7
remove, 37
return, 12
reversed, 49
rjust, 60

script, 21
set, 67
    removal from, 68
sin, 98
slice, 35
    of a string, 46
    of a tuple, 64
sort, 47
sorted, 47
sorting, 47
split, 46
sqrt, 98
stand-alone program, 111

Standard Library, 105
statement, 1
str, 25
string, 1
    finding in another, 46
    format, 56
    joining, 45
    slicing, 46
    splitting, 45
strip, 91
sys, 97

tan, 98
True, 3
try, 77
tuple, 63
    immutability of, 64
    slicing, 64
    unpacking, 63
type, 4
TypeError, 77

unpacking, 63

value, in a dictionary, 65
ValueError, 77

while, 26
with ... as, 58

ZeroDivisionError, 77
zfill, 60
zip, 71

Made in the USA
Monee, IL
13 February 2022

91212184R00131